Mortimer H. Gavin, S.J.

Labor Policy and
Practices in Spain

PRAEGER SPECIAL STUDIES IN
INTERNATIONAL ECONOMICS AND DEVELOPMENT

Labor Policy and Practices in Spain

A STUDY OF EMPLOYER-EMPLOYEE RELATIONS UNDER THE FRANCO REGIME

Fred Witney

Professor of Economics
Indiana University

FREDERICK A. PRAEGER, Publishers
New York · Washington · London

The purpose of the Praeger Special Studies is to make specialized research monographs in international economics and politics available to the academic, business, and government communities. For further information, write to the Special Projects Division, Frederick A. Praeger, Publishers, 111 Fourth Avenue, New York, N. Y. 10003.

FREDERICK A. PRAEGER, PUBLISHERS
111 Fourth Avenue, New York 3, N.Y., U.S.A.
77-79 Charlotte Street, London W.1, England

Published in the United States of America in 1965
by Frederick A. Praeger, Inc., Publishers

Library of Congress Catalog Card Number: 65-27475

Printed in the United States of America

FOREWORD

In the conduct of employer-employee relationships, no question is more basic or more troublesome than the role to be played by government. Societies have been confronted for many years with the decision of the extent to which labor affairs should be subjected to public control. Not unexpectedly, this determination has varied in particular nations according to governmental philosophy, structure, and practices.

Labor relations in Franco Spain, like most other aspects of economic life, have been directly supervised by the state. Professor Witney in this study systematically analyzes how the Spanish government has dominated employer-employee relations for nearly three decades. Largely through labor standards imposed by the Ministry of Labor (<u>reglamentaciones</u>), the Franco government until recent years has permitted relatively little opportunity for labor and management to negotiate freely. Typical of this attitude is the failure of Spain to sign the International Labor Organization's 1948 convention guaranteeing labor the right to join organizations of its own choosing.

A significant feature of the Spanish labor program has been its comprehensive Syndical Organization. Nearly all workers and employers are compulsory, dues-paying members of twenty-eight National Syndicates. Although elected representatives are chosen by the syndicates, neither the authority nor the activities of these organizations are comparable to those of labor unions in modern democracies. Structurally, the Spanish Syndicates bear some resemblance to the corporations which characterized the corporate state of Fascist Italy, but they are entirely devoid of the policy-making functions which resided in the latter.

In recent years the totalitarian labor policies of the Spanish government have been somewhat relaxed. For the first time the right of collective bargaining was recognized in 1958, and by a 1962 decree Spanish workers were granted the right to express lawfully a collective complaint to their employers. Yet, as Professor Witney shows, these do not conclusively point to a meaningful liberalization of regulations; to the contrary, the ordinary labor weapons of picketing, strikes and boycotts are still illegal and compulsory arbitration still prevails.

Perhaps the most important message to be gained from reading this volume may be the implicit warning against vesting absolute power over labor affairs in a national government. Ever since the rise of large, powerful unions in the United States there have been demands for stronger legislative and executive controls, especially during prolonged labor disputes, over employer-employee relations. With the exception of compulsory arbitration during World War II, Congress has largely resisted imposing enforced governmental solutions on strikes, although numerous unfair labor practices have been outlawed and union activities have been regulated.

Professor Witney has made a valuable contribution by his scholarly evaluation of the disadvantages inherent in the restrictive labor policies of Franco Spain. These policies, so vividly portrayed in this book, might well serve as an example which could discourage advocacy of greater national intervention in the labor affairs of our own nation.

Birch Bayh
United States Senator

CONTENTS

PREFACE

This is the story of the Spanish labor relations system under the Franco regime. It begins with the end of the Spanish Civil War, traces its development to the present, and emphasizes the conduct of employer-employee relations under the structure of Spanish labor relations law. As have most other nations, Spain has enacted social welfare laws: laws concerning employment of minors and women, social security, minimum wage and hour provisions, industrial safety and health, apprenticeship regulations, and unemployment compensation. Analysis of their operation, although it would be interesting and informative and would shed additional light on Spain's employment complex, unfortunately falls outside the scope of this study.

Chapter 1 establishes the antecedents for the contemporary labor relations program. Chapter 2 describes the Spanish Syndical Organization, the only employer-employee organization lawful in Spain. This organization, which includes both employers and employees, does not have executive power in the determination of the terms of employment conditions. Still, it is woven into the fabric of Spanish society and has some influence in the labor relations area. Chapter 3 deals with two important elements of contemporary Spanish labor relations--the unlawfulness of strikes and the system of government-imposed minimum labor standards, the system of reglamentaciones. In 1958, Spain enacted a law which for the first time in the Franco era permits a system of collective bargaining. Before this time, employers and employees were not afforded the opportunity to negotiate conditions of employment. These terms were either established by the government through reglamentaciones, the minimum labor standards established by the Ministry of Labor, or by employers, according to conditions prevailing in the labor market. The 1958 law, therefore, marks an important shift in the Spanish labor policy. As Spanish writers put it: "With this law, there is created a new feature to the entire legal structure of Spanish labor. The law of April 24, 1958, established a system of collective contracts for the conditions of work; we may say that it constitutes one of the most fundamental dispositions of the social politics of the nation."[1] In a way, the passage of the 1958 law reflects the kind of excitement stimulated in the United States by the enactment of the Wagner Act. An interpretative analysis of the 1958 law, together with its operation and experience, is highlighted in Chapters 4 and 5. The next chapter evaluates the Spanish collective bargaining system, and the final chapter presents some general conclusions.

Some attempt has been made to describe the framework of the Spanish economic, social, and political environment in which labor relations operate. In so doing, the study highlights some related features of contemporary Spanish society, providing some insight into the socio-economic and political structure of Franco Spain. Also, to gain a perspective of the Spanish collective bargaining system, some comparison is made with United States experience and with a number of basic doctrines of the International Labor Organization.

It is hoped that this study will contribute to the growing store of literature dealing with foreign labor relations problems. In this respect, Spain has been neglected; there is virtually a complete absence of studies in the English language dealing with Spain's labor relations program. A chief purpose for this volume is to fill this gap.

Other considerations made this study appropriate and timely. Currently, important economic, cultural, and military contacts join Spain and the United States. About two hundred American firms operate in Spain, including companies such as United States Steel, Chrysler, Eli Lilly, RCA, Du Pont, and General Electric. As of 1964, American business had invested approximately $153,000,000 in Spanish facilities. That these investments are growing is noted in part by the fact that for 1963 alone, the U. S. business community invested $63,000,000 in the Spanish economy. Each year, approximately 600,000 American tourists visit Spain, and this figure will undoubtedly grow in future years. United States interest in Spain is also evidenced by the fact that in 1964 about 11,000,000 Americans visited the Spanish pavil-

---

[1] José Pérez Leñero, "Convenios Colectivos Sindicales," Revista de Trabajo, Ministerio de Trabajo, v. 7, July, 1958, p. 3, and Jornal, Órgano de Difusión Sindicalista, Organización Sindical Española, Servicio de Relaciones Exteriores, Madrid, No. 80, April-May, 1960, p. 229.

ion at the New York World's Fair. Since 1958, the Fulbright program has been operative in Spain, facilitating an educational exchange program between the two nations. From a modest start in 1958, the number of exchanges steadily increased and currently about two hundred scholars per year are exchanged. Several important United States military bases are located within the Spanish national territory.

During the period 1951 to 1962, the United States conducted an extensive foreign aid program in Spain. Excluding military assistance aid, Spain received $1,173,000,000 under U. S. foreign aid programs. With the improvement in Spanish economic conditions (including gold and foreign exchange reserves, which totalled over one billion dollars in 1964), most U. S. economic aid to Spain terminated in 1962. However, the United States, through the food surplus program and Export-Import Bank loans, in 1963 helped the Spanish economy with programs amounting to about $20,000,000. On the basis of precedent, it can be expected that Spain will obtain increased United States foreign aid if its economy experiences a downturn. In addition, a $524,000,000 expenditure in military aid has been programmed for future years.

In the light of the United States' current relationship to Spain, a study of the labor relations program in that country is appropriate. How are labor relations conducted in Franco Spain? What is the position of the Spanish employer? What are his prerogatives in the conduct of his labor relations program? How does the Spanish government influence those rights? What can the employer do or not do under Spanish labor relations law? What is the position of the Spanish worker? What are his rights, duties, and obligations? How does he fare in a society that outlaws the strike and independent labor unions? Does he receive effective representation from the Spanish Syndical Organization? Has collective bargaining improved his position? In an attempt to achieve meaningful answers to these weighty questions, the study is not only descriptive in character but interpretative and analytical. It is not just a collection of data but rather intends to be a work of sophisticated analysis.

To obtain the raw data for the study, the writer spent approximately six months in Spain, reading extensively about the Spanish labor relations system and conducting more than a score of interviews with Spanish government and Spanish Syndical Organization officials, university faculty members, and labor relations personnel of private firms. Where published material serves as the source for data or analysis, there is appropriate citation. However, the author does not believe that it is convenient or necessary to indicate the source when information has been obtained by personal interview. At this time the author desires to express his sincere gratitude to the many people of Spanish nationality who gave freely of their time in these interviews. Their cooperation was excellent; and, indeed, without their help, this study would not be complete. However, the author wants it perfectly clear that any interpretative comments or conclusions contained in the study are his own responsibility. Opinions, speculations, points of view, and the like are his and his alone. If they are in error, the author alone bears the burden.

Financial support extended by the Ford Foundation through the International Business Studies Program, School of Business, Indiana University, is gratefully acknowledged. The excellent cooperation of the Bureau of Industrial Relations of the International Labor Organization is also duly noted. To his department chairman, Professor Taulman A. Miller, the author is truly indebted for his cooperation in making the time available to execute the study and for his friendly encouragement in this project.

One additional note is worthy though it scarcely deals with the study of labor relations. Whether at the Ministry of Labor, the Spanish Syndical Organization, a private company, the grocery store, the soccer match, the bullfight, on the sidewalk in a workingmen's district or on the fashionable Gran Via, in the bus or street car, the foreign visitor is treated with remarkable sympathy, cooperation, understanding, and courtesy. Here is a quality of the Spanish people which quickly becomes apparent. To these people, the author and his family express their gratitude for a personally pleasant visit to Spain. Spanish people are indeed simpático.

Instead of a dedicatory note, the author hopes that this volume may in some way help the Spanish people secure a rising standard of living. Perhaps it may contribute to this objective. After all, the proper execution of a nation's labor relations program plays a vital part in the well-being of its people.

Fred Witney

Madrid, Spain
December, 1964

Labor Policy and
Practices in Spain

CHAPTER **1** BLUEPRINT FOR
SPAIN'S LABOR
POLICY

LIBERAL-AUTHORITARIANISM

The key to contemporary Spanish labor relations is the
understanding of the phenomenon of an authoritarian state
that in recent years has made an effort to liberalize its institutions.   This development leads to a complex of contradic-
tions within Spain's socio-economic structure, perhaps most
evident in the area of employer-employee relations.   Spain
remains fundamentally an authoritarian state.   This irrefutable proposition stands at the focal point of an inquiry into
its social, political, and economic institutions.   Whatever
elements of liberalization and freedom that exist in contemporary Spain must be viewed within this context.

About the middle of the last decade it became apparent
that Spain could not survive on a self-contained basis; it had
to become integrated economically, socially, and politically
with the Western world.   Spain could not exist in isolation.
With the formation of the United Nations, the European Common Market, the North Atlantic Treaty Organization, and
proposals for a United States of Europe, the pressure to become accepted in the family of Western nations became more
evident. [1]   Indeed, one of the most potent factors in Spain's

---

[1]Spain was admitted into the United Nations in 1952.
As yet, it is not a part of the European Common Market,
though it has made application for membership.   Also, Spain
is not a member of NATO and has not made application for
membership, partly on the expectation that its membership
would be refused because of its totalitarian structure of government.   This would be particularly true of the European
members of NATO, and the 1964 labor victory in England
tends to underscore this proposition.   However, the United
States since 1953 maintains military bases in Spain.   In October, 1964, United States forces, together with Spanish military units, carried out an exercise in the southwest area of
Spain.   It was said that the amphibious feature of the exer-

current wave of liberalization is its desire to be accepted in
the Western community of nations.   There are other factors,
of course, but this one appears to be the most compelling
force behind Spain's effort to relax some elements of totalitarian rule.   Spain seeks to cultivate the West.   From its
phenomenal success at the 1964 New York World's Fair to
its encouragement of scholars of the free world to work in
Spain, the evidence shows clearly that Spain has thrown in its
lot with the West.

Indeed, it is evident that the current Spanish government has passed the point of no return in its effort to inte-
grate with the western community of nations.   Should they
turn their backs on Spain, it is extremely doubtful that the
Franco regime could long survive.   Spain vitally needs economic intercourse with the West.   It must trade with Western
nations, obtain foreign investment, receive tourists, obtain
foreign economic and military aid, and use the West for Spanish worker emigration.

The current policy of liberalization, however, should
not conceal the system of organic totalitarianism which is at
the root of Spanish society.   With the end of the Spanish Civil War, elements of democracy in the short-lived Republic
were swept away.   Francisco Franco became Chief of State
and assumed the powers of a totalitarian ruler.   Despite
Franco's insistence that his powers are "much less important than those conferred upon the President of the United
States through the Constitution of the United States,"[2] the
fact remains that Spain's Caudillo (leader) possesses totalitarian powers.   He has the power to make law on his own
initiative.   His authority was codified by the Spanish Cortes
(Parliament) in 1947.   Thus, "the Chief of State, the leader
of Spain and of the Crusade, is General of the Armies, Francisco Franco Bahamonte."[3]   For his lifetime, Franco is the

---

cise was the largest since the World War II invasion of Nor-
mandy.

[2]Discursos y Mensajes del Jefe del Estado,   1955-
1959, Dirección General de Información Publicaciones Españoles, Madrid, 1960, p. 497.

[3]Ley de Sucesión en La Jefatura del Estado, July
26, 1947, Article II.   (Law of Succession for the Chief of
State).

undeniable leader of Spain.   The Spanish Parliament itself is not elected by popular vote.   Most of its members are appointed by Franco or hold their positions in the Parliament, ex-officio, because they have previous appointive offices in the Spanish government.[4]   It is significant that Franco directly appoints 50 of the Spanish Parliament because of "their positions in the Church, military, administrative, or social agencies, or because of their services to Spain . . . ."[5] The principal function of the Spanish Cortes is to approve legislation presented by the government.   Committees of the Cortes may submit bills to its President, who will place them on an agenda for the government but only if the government agrees.   Further, in practice, no legislation may be enacted without Franco's approval.   In fact, there are no popularly elected political leaders in the Spanish nation. Governors of the 50 Spanish provinces, city mayors, the ministers of the departments of the government, and others who possess law-making powers are appointed.[6]

The circle of Spanish totalitarianism is completed by the injunction contained in the Fuero de Españoles (Law of the Spanish People), enacted by the Spanish Parliament on July 16, 1945, that all "Spanish people must faithfully serve the nation and the Chief of State . . . ."[7] Of interest is the wording of this law which assures the Spanish people of a measure of civil rights.   Spanish citizens, it states, are privileged to "freely express their ideas as long as they do

---

[4]Ley de 17 de Julio de 1945 de Creación de Las Cortes Españoles, Article II.   (Law of July 17, 1945, for the Creation of the Spanish Parliament).

[5]Ibid.

[6]It is true that members of city councils are elected but these bodies do not have the power to enact legislation.   Their powers extend only to the making of recommendations on problems dealing strictly with city administration.   Even these elections are closely controlled.   The appointed mayors within the scope of their jurisdiction may issue legal decrees.   Also, as will be dealt with subsequently, Spanish workers and employers may elect representatives within the Spanish Syndical Organization.

[7]Title I, Chapter I, Article II of the Fuero de Españoles.

not commit a crime against the fundamental principles of the State"; to maintain the secrecy of correspondence; to fix freely their residence within the national territory; to be protected against unlawful entry and search of their homes; to be guarded against unlawful arrest; and to be assured the right of habeas corpus. However, the same law provides that these civil rights may be suspended temporarily by the Spanish government.[8] The Spanish people, therefore, do not possess inalienable, guaranteed, and unassailable civil rights. They may exercise them only to the extent that the Spanish government permits.

Other elements of totalitarianism are evident in contemporary Spanish law. Franco's replacement is already arranged for by the Ley de Sucesión (Law of Succession). He will not be determined by the people in a free election but rather, will be selected by a group from the Cortes. The media of mass communication, the press, radio, and television, are controlled by the State;[9] public meetings may not be held except with the approval of the governors of the provinces;[10] the Falange (national movement) is the only officially recognized political party within Spain and the Chief of State is the ex-officio leader of the Falange;[11] justice dispensed by the Spanish judicial system, though exhibiting more independence than other government institutions, still "must be administered in the name of the Chief of State";[12] and, of particular interest to this study, independent labor organizations and the right to strike do not exist in contemporary Spain.

Such then are the outstanding political elements of the Spanish nation. Although the institutions add up to an author-

---

[8]Title II, Article XXXV.

[9]Ley de 22 de Abril de 1938: Prensa. (Law of April 22, 1938: The Press).

[10]Orden de 20 de Julio de 1939: Reuniones Públicas. (Order of July 20, 1939: Public Meetings).

[11]Decreto de 19 de Abril de 1937. (Decree of April 19, 1937).

[12]Ley de 15 de Septiembre de 1870: Orgánica del Poder Judicial (as amended), Article I. (Law of September 15, 1870: Judicial Power).

itarian-totalitarian state, in recent years there has been considerable liberalization within them. The Spanish people currently enjoy freedoms that seem to contradict the totalitarian structure of the state. For example, unlike residents of the communistic societies, Spanish workers are permitted, and even encouraged, to emigrate to foreign nations. Approximately 350,000 Spanish people are working in Western European nations. [13] Although Catholicism is Spain's official religion, and enjoys protection by the government, [14] Protestants and Jews, who only number about 10,000, may now practice their religion in churches and synagogues. This is a recent development, since Spain's basic law makes public worship of any religion except Catholicism illegal. Despite the official control of the press, the daily newspapers frequently publish criticism of Spanish institutions. True, the line separating tolerated criticism of institutions from that which constitutes a crime against the state is not established with precision. But the fact remains that articles in the daily newspapers are critical of many aspects of Spanish economic and social life. Liberal journals also contain articles critical of various aspects of Spanish institutions. Though most of these journals have a limited circulation, they have a freedom of expression that would not be expected in a totalitarian state. Spanish libraries contain well-stocked collections of foreign volumes, among which are several important American economic and labor journals. The European editions of the New York Times and the New York Herald-Tribune can be purchased without difficulty. In private conversation, Spanish people do not hesitate to make searching appraisals of the basic institutions of the nation, apparently little fearing that such conversations will bring government sanctions against them.

Exposure of the Spanish people to foreign cultures is impressive. Imports of foreign-made goods is an important

---

[13]Luis Alfonso Martínez Cachero, Actualidad de La Emigración Española, Ministerio de Trabajo, Instituto Español de Emigración, Madrid, 1964, p. 14 and "La Emigración Española a Europa," Revista de Información del I. N. I. , Estudios Económicos Información y Síntesis del Instituto, October, 1964, p. 70.

[14]Fuero de Españoles, Title I, Chapter I, Article VI. (Law of the Spanish People).

feature of the Spanish commodity market.   Spanish students
are permitted to study in foreign nations, and students of foreign nations are invited to pursue their studies in Spain.   The
daily press accurately reports economic, cultural, and political developments in foreign nations.   For example, the 1964
U.S. presidential election was displayed prominently in the
Spanish newspapers, radio, and TV.   There was no conceal-
ment of the theory and practice of an election carried out by
a democratic nation.   A large number of U. S. movies and
TV programs, whatever may be their value in interpreting
American institutions, are shown on the Spanish TV network
and in its theaters.   An important Spanish policy is to encourage tourism.   Indeed, in 1963, about 9 million tourists visited Spain, a figure which placed Spain just below Italy as the
most popular tourist attraction in Europe.[15]   Tourists enter
Spain with no difficulty, and the Spanish government has established a variety of measures to provide assistance and
protection to foreign tourists.   Though Spain's encouragement of tourists, of course, has an economic basis, the fact
still remains that the cultural heritage of the foreign visitor
is bound to rub off on the Spanish people.

In short, within the context of a totalitarian state, the
Spanish people currently are enjoying a measure of liberty.
As in all dictatorships, this development presents a basic
dilemma to the Spanish government.   Once the fresh air of
freedom has wafted through the window, the government cannot slam it shut.   To do so undoubtedly would result in a public convulsion that would carry with it the strongest of political consequences.   On the other hand, the taste of freedom,
however faint, provokes a thirst for more liberty.   Significant additional freedoms could be a powerful force in a radi-
cal change in the basic political structure.

Within this framework a meaningful inquiry into the
contemporary state of Spanish labor relations must be made.
As the study develops, the conflict between totalitarianism
and freedom becomes evident.   Spanish labor relations reflect the current turbulence in Spain's political and institu-

---

[15]Arriba (Madrid), November 1, 1964.   Estimates for
1964 will place tourism in Spain above the 13,000,000 mark.
(The Spanish daily press is an excellent source of information for legal decrees and policies announced by the Spanish
government.   Thus, citations will be made to leading Spanish
newspapers such as Arriba, Ya, ABC, and Pueblo).

tional life.   There are elements of freedom and totalitarianism--manifestations of self-determination and of state control.   It will be stated at the outset that in the area of labor relations, state control has an overwhelming edge over self-determination.   Still, certain elements of freedom are unmistakable.

ANTECEDENTS OF CURRENT
SPANISH LABOR POLICY

The blueprint for much of Spain's contemporary labor relations system was laid out during the era of the Republic. Its architect, José Antonio Primo de Rivera, viewed the labor function as an organic and integrated element of a totalitarian-syndical state. [16]   José Antonio, founder of the Falange, was the author of the basic tenets of the Spanish state.   Rejecting a society based on either capitalistic liberalism or socialism, he advocated for Spain a state "which is not of the left or the right.   Because fundamentally the right aspires to maintain an unjust economic organization. And the left has its desire to undermine an economic system, although its destruction would carry with it the destruction of many good values.   The nation is a total unity in which are integrated all the individuals and all classes; the nation should not be in the hands of the strongest classes or in the hands of the best organized party.   The nation is a synthesis, an indivisible synthesis with its own ends and objectives. And what we want is that the Movement (Falange) will establish a State that will be an effective instrument, authoritarian, for permanent and irrevocable unity."[17]   Undoubtedly,

---

[16]José Antonio Primo de Rivera was the son of Migüel Primo de Rivera who was established as the Dictator of Spain under the reign of Alphonso XIII, the last king of the nation. He served as the dictator of Spain from 1923 until 1929 when the Spanish Republic was established. José Antonio was killed in November, 1936,while fighting with the Franco forces.   He was 33 years old at the time of his death.

[17]Obras Completas de José Antonio Primo de Rivera, Delegación de Prensa y Propoganda de Falange Española Tradicionalista y de las J. O. N. S. , Madrid, 1942, p. 17.

José Antonio was profoundly influenced by Mussolini's fascist Italy.   At one time he rejected the idea that Italian fasc-
ism would terminate with the death of Mussolini.   Conceding
that with the death of Mussolini Italy would undergo a short
period of "anxiety," he nevertheless claimed that the fascist
system would produce another leader--"and this chief will
perpetuate this system for many years."[18]
     An authoritarian state cannot tolerate organizations
that promote the interests of particular economic classes.
That is, within a totalitarian state all members and groups
are to be subordinated to the state's higher interest. Consequently, there is no place for independent labor unions or
employer organizations.   Such a philosophy holds that as the
different economic interests are subordinated for the good of
the state, their particular interests will be advanced.   Thus,
José Antonio stated: ". . . we (the Falange) view Spain, on
the economic side, as a gigantic syndicate of workers. We
shall organize a Spanish society through a system of vertical
syndicates based upon branches of production dedicated to
the service of an integrated national economy.   The national-
syndical state shall not cruelly inhibit the economic struggle
between men.   Our regime shall make impossible the struggle between classes because all who cooperate in production
constitute a total organism."[19]

EXECUTION OF THE BLUEPRINT

     With the end of the Spanish Civil War, the blueprint of
José Antonio's labor policy was translated into action.   On
January 26, 1940, the Spanish government enacted its Ley de
Unidad Sindical (Law of Syndical Unity).   This law proclaimed that all factors of the economy are to be enclosed
within a national syndicate structure according to each
branch of production or service.   At the same time the law
abolished and made illegal all existing labor unions and em-

Contained in a speech made on October 29, 1933, in the Tea-
tro de la Comedia, Madrid.

[18]Ibid., p. 406.

[19]Ibid., p. 468.

ployer associations.

Prior to the Franco regime in Spain two major labor union groups existed--the Confederación Nacional del Trabajo (National Confederation of Labor) and the Unión General de Trabajadores (General Union of Workers). The CNT was established in 1910 and the UGT in 1888.[20] Some contemporary Spanish writers claim these organizations were oriented more to political goals than to the function of trade unionism, and charge that they engaged in serious acts of violence and public disorder. Thus, the CNT and the UGT "founded with noble ends were converted into instruments of political struggle at the service of those factions which inspired them. Outrages, strikes, arson, devastations, crimes, and all classes of excesses which marked the development of the Spanish labor movement . . . are eloquent landmarks which demonstrated the clear aberration of Spanish unionism."[21]

Another point of view is that the pre-Franco trade union movement strived unsuccessfully for recognition and social approbation. Its failure to be accepted fully as an integral part of Spanish society tends to explain some of its excesses.

These labor bodies, as well as all other elements of pre-Franco trade unionism, were abolished. The Law of Syndical Unity states: "The Syndical Organization is the only one recognized with sufficient legality by the State, which will not admit the existence of any other [labor or employer association] with analagous or similar goals. . . ."[22] It provides further that "those associations created in order to defend or represent economic or class interests, called unions, associations, guilds, etc., will be incorporated in the Syndical Organization." These words sounded the death knell for the free Spanish trade union movement and of collective bargaining. In their place was established the Organización Sindical Española (Spanish Syndical Organization), to which Spanish workers and employers are compelled to be-

---

[20]G. Bayón Chacón and E. Pérez Botija, Manual de Derecho del Trabajo, Madrid, 1964, p. 713.

[21]Capacitación Sindical, Organización Sindical Española, Centro de Estudios Sindicales, Madrid, 1960, p. 20.

[22]Article I.

long. It would be as if the United States abolished all independent labor organizations and employer associations and created in their place, by law, a new monolithic organization,
requiring membership of all American employees and employers.

AN INSTRUMENT OF STATE POLICY

The structure and goals of the Spanish Syndical Organization were outlined in a law enacted on December 6, 1940.[23]
That the Spanish Syndical Organization is a creature of the
state and was established to carry out the policies of the Spanish government is clearly stated in the preamble to this law:
". . . This law assures the subordination of the syndical organization to the Party (Falange) and only this Party can establish the discipline, the unity and the spirit necessary for
the national economy to serve national policy." In short, the
Falange, the only political party permitted in Spain, will control the operation of the syndicate organization. As the Falange is dedicated to further the interest of the Spanish state,
it is irrefutable that the syndicate system is likewise an instrument of the Spanish government.

To further establish this point is a declaration in the
Fuero de Trabajo (Rights of Labor). The Rights of Labor constitutes a basic set of principles in the labor and economic
field that were promulgated by the Falange on March 9, 1938.
In 1947 the Rights of Labor was elevated to the status of a
fundamental law of Spain.[24] It states: "The vertical [includ-
ing employers and employees] syndical system is an instrument to the service of the State, through which it [the State]
shall realize, principally, its economic policy."

Despite these declarations, and despite the fact that all
policy-making jobs within the organization are filled by appointment by the Spanish government,[25] syndical leaders,

---

[23]La Ley de Bases de La Organización Sindical. (Law
for the Bases of Syndical Organization).

[24]Ley de Sucesión en La Jefatura del Estado, July 16,
1947, Article X. (Law of Succession for the Chief of State).

[25]Chapter 2 treats this issue in fuller detail.

who hold their jobs at the pleasure of the government, repeatedly assert that the syndical organization is independent from the Spanish government and that it truly and realistically represents the goals of its members. They argue that the organization is the authentic representative of workers and employers because it effectively represents them unhampered by government control. For example, the appointed and highest officer of the organization, claims: ". . . we are weary of being told of the lack of authenticity, because we know that those who talk this way do not know of the vivid reality of your presence . . . ."[26] Such a point of view is contrary to the facts and is in direct opposition to the laws which have established the Spanish syndicate system. The inescapable conclusion must be that the syndicate system is an organism of the Spanish government and will remain so until its members have the right to elect all officers regardless of rank. Further, to cut the cord which currently ties the system to the government, employers and employees must be free from compulsion to belong and to pay dues to the organization.

It must be noted that not all Spanish people accept the organization's statement that it is an authentic representative of its members and is free from state control. In a critical article dealing with aspects of Spain's labor relations problems, (which incidentally tends to demonstrate the measure of freedom of expression the Spanish people now enjoy)

---

[26]"Trade Union Elections," National Assembly of Trade Union Elections, Spanish National Syndical Organization, Madrid, 1963, p. 2. (A few references discovered by this author are in the English language. Where this occurs, the English citation is used.) This statement was made to a group of 9,000 elected syndical employer and employee representatives. Every three years the Spanish Syndical Organization holds elections designed to provide representation to the employers and employees within the structure. More will be said of these elections later in this study. At this place it suffices to point out that despite these elections, the fact remains that all policy-making jobs which carry executive power are filled through appointment by the Spanish government. In fact, a former Secretary General of the syndical organization, the second highest job in the structure, was removed from office when he advocated that some of these officials be freely elected by employees and employers.

a Spanish author concludes: ". . . we continue to think that
under an economic system of neo-capitalism[27] in which we
live, the only way of opposing the power of business will be
the organization of all workers in authentic unions of their
own."[28]   An observation by another contemporary Spanish
writer is also revealing: Spanish "unionism has been converted to be an instrument of the state to promote the reali-
zation of its economic policy,"[29] and other writers take issue with the proposition that the representation of workers
by the Spanish syndical organization is free from state domination.   In view of the fundamental laws that chart the basic
structure, government, and operation of the syndicate system, it is impossible for an independent and objective apprais-
al to arrive at any other conclusion.

This subordination to the government violates an important standard of the International Labor Organization.   In
1956, Spain resumed its membership in the ILO after having
dropped out during the early years of the Franco regime.   In
1962, the ILO adopted a resolution concerning "the Independence of the Trade Union Movement."   Paragraph 6 of the
resolution provides:

> . . . governments in seeking the cooperation of
> trade unions to carry out their economic and soc-
> ial policies should recognize that the value of this
> cooperation rests to a large extent on the freedom

[27]Spain's economic system is based upon free enterprise.   The vast number of companies are privately owned.
Prices are established by the market, though the criticism
exists that in many areas there is a great deal of private monopoly.   Indeed, the aforecited Rights of Labor states: "The
State recognizes private initiative as the fruitful source of the
economic life of the nation; and the State recognizes and pro-
tects private property as the natural means for the fulfillment
of individual, family, and social functions."

[28]Julian Ariza Ricoi, "Convenios Colectivos," Cuadernos Para El Diálogo, Madrid, No. 10-11, July-August, 1964,
p. 9.

[29]Jacinto Martín, "Cincuenta Años de Vida Sindical,"
Cuadernos Para El Diálogo, Madrid, No. 9, June, 1964, p.
11.

and independence of the trade union movement as an essential factor in promoting social advancement and should not attempt to transform the trade union movement into an instrument for the pursuance of political aims, nor should they attempt to interfere with the normal functions of a trade union movement because of its freely established relationship with a political party.

These reports show clearly that the Spanish Syndical Organization fails to measure up to the principles established in this ILO resolution. The <u>Falange</u> is the only political party authorized in Spain. Under <u>Spain's</u> law, the Basis of Syndical Organization, it is provided that the <u>Falange</u> exercises supervisory control of the Spanish Syndical Organization. It is equally manifest that in its inception the syndical organization was created as "an instrument to the service of the State" and through which the Spanish government implements its economic objectives. That the organization continues as a servant of the Spanish government will be much more obvious in subsequent portions of this volume. The discussion dealing with the wage control policy announced by the Spanish government on November 20, 1964, is of particular importance in this respect.

CHAPTER **2** THE SPANISH SYNDICAL ORGANIZATION

It is clear that the Spanish Syndical Organization is the only legal Spanish employer-employee movement. With the exception of a few groups of workers, (about 450,000 domestic servants and about 500,000 public employees) all Spanish employees and employers are compelled to belong to the syndicate organization. In 1964, membership constituted about 9 million workers and 3.3 million employers.[1] At the same time, the Spanish labor force amounted to about 13 million; the total national population, approximately 31 million. Of the entire labor force, therefore, about 92 per cent belong to the Spanish Syndical Organization. Each employee is compelled to pay dues of 0.3 of 1 per cent of his basic salary, and employers must contribute 1.5 per cent of their basic payrolls. Accordingly, for 1964, the total revenue of the syndicate organization amounted to about $45.8 million.

BASIC STRUCTURE

Spain's employers and employees currently are divided into 28 national syndicate organizations, each of which covers a broad sector of the economy.[2] At the apex of the national

---

[1]"Trade Union Elections," National Assembly of Trade Union Elections, Spanish National Syndical Organization, Madrid, 1963, p. 1.

[2]At present there is a national syndicate for each of the following industries: banks and stock exchanges; cattle; cereal; chemicals; coal and combustible fuels; construction, glass, and ceramics; diverse activities; entertainment; farmers, farm workers, and breeders; fishing; food; fruits and farm products; gas, water, and electricity; hotels, insurance; leather; merchant marine; metal; olive oil; paper, press, and graphic arts; private teachers; radio, TV, and the press; sanitary personnel; sugar; textiles; transportation and communication; wine, beer, and beverages; wood and cork.

syndicates is the Delegación Nacional de Sindicatos (National
Delegation of Syndicates), to which all the national syndicate
organizations must belong.   It is the coordinating and controlling unit of the entire Spanish Syndical Organization.   Its
two chief officers are the Delegado Nacional (National Delegate) and the Secretario General (Secretary-General).   Within
the national office are located a variety of units, two of which
are of particular importance.   One unit is the "social" or
workers' section and the other the "economic" or employers'
section.   Each of these sections is headed by a Vicesecretario
Nacional (National Vice-Secretary).   In short, the national
body is divided into two functional sections--one for the
workers and the other for employers.   The employers' section is charged with the general responsibility of representing
the employer interests; the workers' section, with the general
responsibility of representing the workers' interests.   Any
conflict between the two sections at the national level can be
resolved by the Secretary-General or the National Delegate.

Each of the 28 National Syndicates is headed by a so-
called "President."   Like the National Delegation of Syndicates, each national syndicate is divided into worker and employer sections.   Each establishes lower level syndicate units
--provincial, city, or county and all the syndicates in each
of the 50 provinces are tied together into a provincial syndical unit.   At the head of each province is a Delegado Provincial (Provincial Delegate) and within each are many additional
groupings of syndical units.   Also, there are syndical units
at the plant level.

It is stressed that each syndicate includes all employers
and employees covered by its jurisdiction, and they are compelled to belong to their respective syndicates.   Each syndicate unit, regardless of rank, is divided into a worker and employer section.   It is of crucial importance that the line of
authority is from top to the bottom.   Through a network of
appointed officers, policies may be implemented from the
highest level down through the provincial and local levels.   In
a way, the Spanish Syndical Organization resembles the theoretical structure of the Knights of Labor wherein the component parts of the organization did not possess the autonomy
needed for independent action.

As of 1964 there were 14, 189 local syndicate units,
1, 300 syndical bodies which operated in the provinces, and
the 28 national syndicate organizations.[3]   All of the officers

---

"Trade Union Elections," op. cit., p. 1.

in the national body, the one hundred or so important leaders of the national syndicates, and about two hundred syndical officials who head the syndical groupings at provincial levels, including the 50 provincial chiefs, hold their offices by appointment. They are appointed either directly by Franco, or by appointees of Franco. Each appointed officer has the authority to execute, within his jurisdiction, the policies of the Spanish Syndical Organization.

SYNDICAL ELECTIONS

Who then is elected by the employers and the employees? What authority do they possess? Every three years the workers and the employers in the various syndicates have the opportunity to elect representatives. The elections are secret, and, apparently, all members are entitled to vote. Certain technical qualifications are attached to being nominated and to holding office, such as Spanish nationality, age, literacy, and seniority within the firm.[4] It is difficult to determine whether or not any person who meets the basic technical qualifications may be nominated or elected to office. One qualification for holding office states: ". . . fulfill the required conditions of legal, moral and professional aptitude according to the legislation in force."[5] Under such vague, general, and broad language, it appears quite possible that the syndicates that administer the election laws can easily veto the nomination or election of a person for a variety of reasons. Any person could be declared persona non grata because of economic, political, or social beliefs or disapproved activities. The existence of this implicit veto power is difficult to prove, but if it did not exist, the election laws would be written in a manner that would guarantee to the workers and employers absolute free choice to nominate and elect whomever they desire, free from any control by the syndicate organization.

In any event, in the elections of 1963, the Spanish Syndical Organization announced that workers elected about 175, 000

---

[4]General Regulations for Trade Union Elections, Spanish Trade Union Organization, Madrid, 1963, p. 11.

[5]Ibid., p. 14.

representatives, and employers elected more than 233,000. The lowest level elected worker representative, an "enlace", would compare roughly in function to an American shop steward. The lowest level of employer elected officers are designated as members of local economic boards. Workers and employers directly elect representatives to the lower level elected posts, who are then eligible for election to higher positions. In these higher office elections, in general, only those who have been elected previously may vote and be elected to the more important positions. For example, only shop stewards may be elected to plant labor-management committees.

Shop stewards carry out the following major duties: (1) advise workers on their social and labor rights; (2) support workers' claims with either employer or syndicate groups; (3) maintain workers' interests in social, labor, and syndicate affairs; (4) carry out specific missions assigned to the workers in their plants by their syndical leaders; and (5) represent workers in collective bargaining.[6]

While the workers in every firm, regardless of size, have the opportunity to elect stewards, only workers in firms with a labor force of 100 or more are afforded the opportunity to elect representatives to labor-management committees.[7] In short, labor-management committees do not exist in firms of less than 100 workers, while in those of 100 or more employees such a body must be in existence. In general, the worker members of labor-management committees perform the following major functions: (1) propose to employers methods to increase output of the quality of the product; (2) report complaints of workers to the employer; (3) administer their firm's social welfare funds; (4) represent the workers in collective bargaining; and (5) participate with the employer in the drafting of their firm's internal labor regulations.[8] The num-

---

[6]"El Enlace Sindical," Organización Sindical Española, Vicesecretaria Nacional de Ordenación Social, Madrid, 1963, pp. 5-26.

[7]Decreto del Ministerio de Trabajo, September 11, 1953. (Decree of the Minister of Labor).

[8]The latter function requires some explanation. Under Spanish labor law, each firm with more than 50 permanent employees must file with the Ministry of Labor a set of rules

ber of worker members on the labor-management committees depends upon the size of the enterprise. For example, plants with 100 to 250 workers have four worker representatives. However, the Ministry of Labor decree establishing the system of labor-management committees requires that the employer or his representative serve as the President of the group.

The powers extended to elected worker representatives make it apparent that they are not authorized to compel any positive action on the part of the employer. At the best, their powers are merely consultive or advisory. As developed below, their powers in the area of collective bargaining are limited by the fact that any agreements achieved by them are subject to the approval or disapproval of the Ministry of Labor. Furthermore, the elected representatives of the Spanish Syndical Organization are subordinate to the appointed officials. They may counsel, advise, or even argue their point of view with appointed syndical officials; however, it is clear that at points of showdown, the appointed syndical representatives will have their way.

The fact that the elected representatives are far more numerous than the appointed representatives is irrelevant in this connection. The important factor is who holds the power to carry out policies, notwithstanding the declaration of a former Secretary-General of the Spanish Syndical Organization, Francisco Giménez Torres, who states: "Out of the 400,000 official positions in our union movement, only about 80 are appointed; all the rest are subject to the electoral machinery."[9] His figure of 80 appointed representatives is much too low.

---

to govern working conditions in the plant. This code covers working conditions such as wages, vacations, holidays, discipline, promotions, rest periods, etc. The Ministry of Labor will approve or disapprove such submitted codes. Working conditions so established may not be less favorable than those established by the Ministry of Labor, under the regla- mentaciones system, a subject with which we will be concerned subsequently. See Manual del Dirigente de Empresa, Organización Sindical Española, Vicesecretaria Nacional de Ordenación Económica, Madrid, 1964, pp. 519-522.

[9] Francisco Giménez Torres, "The Objectives of Spanish Unions," Organización Sindical Española, Servicio de Relaciones Exteriores Sindicales, Madrid, 1962, p. 8.

Moreover, what makes his statement misleading is the fact that Torres himself was relieved from his office partly on the grounds that he advocated subjecting to the elective process some important jobs now filled by appointment.

THEORY AND FUNCTION

In the Spanish labor relations field, the destruction of independent labor unions and employer associations, and the forging together of employers and employees in the same group is supposed to achieve a state of affairs wherein labor problems will be resolved harmoniously and fairly for the benefit of the employees, the employers, the industry, and the nation. Conflicts that arise will be settled within the "family" and the result will be peace and justice. When the employer and employee sections fail to resolve their disputes by themselves, they can call upon the judgment of the appointed President of a syndicate, and, if necessary, the high officers of the National Delegation of Syndicates. Because these people are assumed to have superior wisdom and to be endowed with a special facility to dispense justice, it is supposed that their decisions will be readily accepted by the combatants-- accepted not as a matter of force, but because of the quality and equity of the decisions.

Such a theory must be evaluated on the basis of several fundamental considerations. In the first place, if the syndical system really possesses the quality of harmony of interest, the question arises as to why the Spanish government outlaws strikes. It would appear that strikes would not be necessary if the syndical system could effectively achieve this harmony. Further, since 1939 many illegal strikes have taken place in Spain. As recently as 1962, 1963, and 1964, waves of bitterly contested strikes occurred in the northern part of the nation. Unfortunately, no evidence is available to determine accurately the number of strikes and their duration, the number of workers involved in these illegal strikes, and the man-days lost to production. The Spanish government does not make such data available. That the figure would be considerable is conceded by several informed observers of the Spanish scene.

With no assurance of unquestioned accuracy sources in Spain report that from 80,000 to 100,000 Spanish workers were involved in strikes in 1962. In 1963 the figure was somewhat lower, and in the spring of 1964 strike activity included

40,000 workers. As in previous years, the major locale of the 1964 strikes was in the Asturias coal mining area. Asturias is a northern province of Spain and is Spain's largest coal producing center. Indeed, the 1964 strikes in this area marked the fourth major work stoppage in 1963-1964. The audacious and fearless character of the Asturian miners sticks as a bone in the throat of the Spanish government and the syndical organization. Should independent unions and the right to strike return to Spain, it will be largely attributable to these workers. Among the demands of the Asturian miners in 1964 were higher wages, improved working conditions, the right to strike, and independent unions. As a commentary on the inability of the Spanish Syndical Organization to handle labor relations problems, the strike terminated only after the Spanish government, through the Ministry of Labor, ordered the owners to pay a significant increase in wages to the striking workers. Some repressive measures were used to terminate the strike, including some arrests, but the back-to-work movement was mainly induced by the wage increase. Naturally, the Spanish government refused demands to legalize strikes and independent unions; to do so would mean the end of the Spanish Syndical Organization as currently constituted, with obvious implications for the Franco regime.

For two reasons, the government's handling of the 1964 strikes seems to be defeating its own best interests. The capitulation of the Spanish government tends to reinforce workers' confidence in their own strength. Furthermore, negotiation was effected not through the Spanish Syndical Organization but with leaders in whom the workers had confidence. In short, to terminate the strike, the Spanish Syndical Organization was bypassed.

As a further weakness, the Spanish Syndical Organization does not have the power to determine working conditions. It may make proposals to the Ministry of Labor, but only the latter has the ultimate power to determine wages and working conditions. If it were true that the "harmonizing" concept of the syndicate system works in practice, then it would follow that the Spanish government would entrust this important function to the syndicates. Even in the area of collective bargaining, the syndicates play a secondary role with respect to the determination of working conditions established in collective agreements. Though the agreements are negotiated within the network of the syndicate system, the Ministry of Labor has the ultimate power over the collective bargaining agreements. It is indeed significant that though the syndicates are designed to carry out government policy and are realistically a branch of the Spanish government, they have not been entrusted with the function of the determination of working conditions.

Some Spanish workers understand that the Spanish Syndical Organization cannot represent them effectively.   An unknown number of workers, largely in the northern industrial provinces, have joined clandestine Roman Catholic labor organizations that do not admit employers. The Spanish government is aware of their existence, but since the Roman Catholic Church is a significant power center in Spanish society and constitutes a pillar of the Franco regime, the government fears to attack and destroy such illegal bodies.

Indeed, from time to time, the Spanish government itself, aware of the restlessness of workers, recognizes in a semi-official way that the Spanish Syndical Organization does not authentically represent workers. In the fall of 1964, the National Delegate of the Spanish Syndical Organization spoke in terms of establishing a series of workers' councils to express with greater authority grievances and aspirations of the Spanish workers. [10] On October 23, 1964, Ministry of Labor representatives and syndical organization officials participated in high-level talks, suggesting establishment of a broad labor front as a forum for presenting exclusive worker demands to the Spanish government. [11] Such labor bodies would operate within the Spanish Syndical Organization.

However, as long as the Spanish Syndical Organization remains in its present form, these groups cannot do much more than attempt to siphon off some worker discontent to forestall the formation of independent labor unions.   In short, the dilemma facing the Spanish government is this: Although it knows that the Spanish Syndical Organization does not effectively represent the Spanish workers, the government realizes that the formation of authentic and independent labor organizations would threaten the very existence of the Franco regime.

On the basis of these observations, it is quite clear that the Spanish Syndical Organization simply does not have the capacity for effective representation of workers' interests in labor relations, since its primary assumption is a philosoph-

---

[10]Ya (Madrid), November 7, 1964.

[11]New York Times (American Edition), October 25, 1964.

ical impossibility in the context of a capitalistic state. It assumes that both workers and employers in such an economy will subordinate their own basic interests in favor of some mythical superior objective; that is, the support of a society in which as by magic workers and employers would cease to think and act as themselves. This assumption is a self-delusion.

What then are the essential functions of the Spanish Syndical Organization? What is its role in the affairs of the nation? Its economic or employer section has the following major functions: to study and discuss problems affecting the nation's economy; to be in touch with the various ministries of the Spanish government (labor, commerce, public works, finance, etc.); to discuss with the ministries and advise them of possible solutions to economic problems; and to represent the employers' interests in this context. The social or the workers' section represents workers in the recommendation and development of programs leading to the improvement of workers' living conditions through better housing; health programs; unemployment measures; and the sponsorship of a wide range of recreational and educational facilities. The latter function deserves special comment. The Spanish Syndical Organization, largely through its social section, carries out a broad range of activities designed to improve the workers' lot. At the present time, it operates 112 vocational training schools with over 30,000 registered students. Also, the organization provides free legal services for Spanish workers involved in litigation before special Spanish labor courts. In addition, the organization sponsors a wide variety of sport activities, operates impressive vacation resorts at small cost to Spanish workers, and publishes a Madrid daily newspaper and many books and pamphlets on economic, social, and labor matters.

Therefore, although the Spanish Syndical Organization carries out a wide variety of important social activities, it is not designed to play an effective role in the area of labor relations. In the United States, where social welfare programs are implemented through community, state, and federal governments, or by private associations, an independent labor movement through the process of collective bargaining plays a vital part in the determination of working conditions. How the Spanish Syndical Organization is involved in Spain's contemporary collective bargaining program is the subject of later analysis. Even in this respect, it will be shown that the organization plays a secondary role in the determination of working conditions.

Indeed, it is understandable that Spain, to this date, has never signed International Labor Organization Convention Number 87 concerning the "Freedom of Association and Protection of the Right to Organize," adopted by the ILO in 1948. It states, in part, that

> Workers and employers, without distinction whatsoever, shall have the right to establish and, subject only to the rules of the organization concerned, to join organizations of their own choosing without previous authorization. Worker and employer organizations shall have the right to draw up their constitutions and rules, to elect their representatives in full freedom, to organize their administration and activities and to formulate their programs. The public authorities shall refrain from any interference which would restrict this right or impede the lawful exercise thereof.

The Spanish Syndical Organization violates the letter and spirit of this fundamental doctrine. Neither Spanish employers nor workers are free to join organizations of their own choosing. They are forced to belong to the Spanish Syndical Organization and pay to it compulsory dues. Rules and constitution of the Spanish syndicate system cannot be freely adopted by employers and employees. Through the network of appointed representatives, the Spanish government in truth has the final power to dictate the rules and objectives of the Spanish Syndical Organization.

CHAPTER **3** RIGHT TO STRIKE
AND MINIMUM LABOR
STANDARDS

STRIKES ILLEGAL

Strikes are unlawful in Spain according to a policy established in the Rights of Labor, adopted by the Spanish Falange, and enacted into law by Franco in 1938. Under the terms of Article XI, Paragraph 2 of this fundamental law, "individual or collective acts which in any manner disturb the normality of production shall be considered as crimes against the State." Subsequently, Article 222 of Spain's penal code treats strikes and lockouts as criminal sedition and provides appropriate penal sanctions for workers who engage in these forms of industrial conflict. [1] Since March 24, 1943, strikes which have a "political" purpose are considered as a military rebellion; workers who participate in them are subject to trial and conviction under military tribunals, rather than the civil authority. [2]

That these prohibitions against the strike are not only academic is clearly established by a government declaration involving the 1962 Asturias' coal strikes. A minister of Franco's cabinet attributed the strikes to the actions of "agitators" who were "aided and abetted by foreign sources."[3] His statement complains further that "it is deplorable that a

---

[1]G. Bayón Chacón and E. Pérez Botija, Manual de Derecho del Trabajo, Madrid, 1964, p. 782.

[2]José Alvarez de Miranda, "Conflictos Colectivos Laborales," Cuadernos, Organización Sindical Española, Centro de Estudios Sindicales, Madrid, No. 20, June, 1963, p. 166.

[3]Revista de Trabajo, Ministerio de Trabajo, Madrid, No. 3, June, 1962, p. 1038.

sane majority of Asturias' workers may be torn down by an insidious campaign, disorienting their opinion and judgment, which has occasioned a costly sacrifice to the workers affected and a grave danger to the national economy--a basic objective of those who desire to obstruct our policy of constant social and economic improvement." The fact that coal miners were earning about $1.51 per day in 1962[4] apparently was not considered by the government as the motivating factor for the strikes. Striking employees were warned during the course of the strikes that "the government affirms its firm purpose of dedicating all its attention to the establishment of labor normality, applying vigorously the norms of discipline using the means that current legislation authorizes for the maintenance of social defense, order, and peace."[5]

Also pertinent is the treatment of a group of Spanish workers who were involved in the coal strikes of 1963. This account appeared in the European edition of the New York Herald-Tribune on November 19, 1964:

> The government today brought to trial 30 miners and one woman accused of taking part in strikes in northern Asturias last year.
>
> The defendants, if convicted, could draw sentences of up to ten years in jail.
>
> Seven of the defendants were brought from the Carabanchel prison to the court. All the others were released on 'provisional liberty' until the time of the trial after spending eight months in jail.
>
> The defendants told newsmen before the trial started that they had been 'tortured' by members of the Guardia Civil (rural police).

The same newspaper a week later reported that most of the accused were sentenced to a year in jail, while four, including the woman, were acquitted.

---

[4]Anuario Estadístico de España, Presidencia del Gobierno, Instituto Nacional de Estadística, Madrid, 1963, p. 258.

[5]Revista de Trabajo, op. cit., p. 1038.

SPANISH GOVERNMENT INDICTED IN THE ILO

Upon occasion, charges have been filed with the International Labor Organization against the Spanish government for its treatment of strikers. For example, the International Confederation of Free Trade Unions, the International Federation of Christian Trade Unions, and the World Federation of Trade Unions complained that the Spanish government arrested strikers, forced them to reside in certain localities within the nation, discharged them from their jobs, and tortured some of them. These charges, based upon the action of the Spanish government during the 1962 and 1963 strikes, were submitted to the ILO Committee on Freedom of Association. [6] In part, the charges complained of the imprisonment of 47 Spanish workers who participated in the 1962 strikes. When asked by the ILO to report on the status of these workers, the Spanish government replied on July 29, 1963, that it had "amnestied a number of the 47 persons and reduced the sentence on some of the others. "[7] The Spanish government, however, refused to supply to the ILO the judgment of the courts that sentenced these workers to jail. These judgments were requested to determine the factual basis for the arrests and the reasoning of the Spanish courts for their decisions. The ILO Committee on Freedom of Association regretted that the Spanish government "maintains its decision not to furnish the texts of the judgments rendered in the cases of the 47 persons. . . emphasizing that the actual texts of the judicial decisions afford much clearer evidence of the fact that the preceedings taken have no relation to trade union activities. "[8] Previously, the Spanish government refused to make available the judgment of the courts on the grounds that their "case involved a matter of principle because the said judgments did not concern workers or trade union unionists as such or because of their participation in industrial disputes. "[9] Instead, the Spanish government

---

[6]Official Bulletin, International Labor Office, Geneva, V. 47, No. 3, Supplement II, July, 1964, pp. 58-65.

[7]Ibid., p. 58.

[8]Ibid., p. 60.

[9]Ibid., p. 59.

contended that the arrested workers sought to overthrow the regime, and, therefore, their activities did not reflect trade unionism. It alleged further that some of the arrested strikers were known communists. In the absence of the texts of the judgment, it is impossible to determine with accuracy whether or not the imprisoned workers were merely engaging in normal and accepted trade union practices or were imprisoned because of communist affiliation and efforts to overthrow the Spanish government. If the latter were true, it would follow that the Spanish government would not hesitate to make the court judgment available to the public. That it continues to withhold the judgment seems to indicate that the true facts of the case are being concealed. The character of the oppressive measures of the Spanish government towards strikes is also made evident by the fact that in 1962 it caused "the dismissal of many strikers, with loss of their acquired rights and benefits when they were re-engaged."[10]

With respect to the charge of compulsory residence, the ICFTU and the IFCTU contended that the Spanish government subjected "certain participants in the Asturian strikes of 1962 to compulsory residence orders . . . ."[11] By this measure, the Spanish government forcibly moves striking workers from one part of Spain to another. For example, it will move a worker and his family from a northern province to the southern area of the nation and compel them to reside in the new locality for a certain period of time. It would be as if the United States government would forcibly transport striking workers from Chicago to Mississippi. When requested to reply to such allegations, the Spanish government replied on February 10, 1964, that "all the compulsory residence orders referred to in previous communications were due to activities involving the organization of, or incitement to, subversion in an attempt to seize control of a peaceful industrial dispute for political purposes of patently seditious intent."[12] As stated earlier in this volume, the Law of the Spanish people (Fuero de Españoles) guaranteed the right of the Spanish people "to fix freely their residence within the national territory," but that under the same law the Spanish gov-

---

[10]Ibid., p. 60.

[11]Ibid., p. 60.

[12]Ibid., p. 61.

ernment may suspend any of the civil rights guarantees. This is what occurred during the 1962 strikes, for on June 8, 1962, the Spanish government '"temporarily' suspended some of the guarantees of the said fundamental law (Fuero de Españoles)."[13] Actually, the Spanish government suspended that right of free location of residence throughout the whole nation for a period of two years.[14] This action of the Spanish government underscores the previous proposition that Spanish people enjoy civil rights only to the extent that their government permits their exercise; they may be suspended at any time.

With respect to the 1963 strikes, some spokesmen charge that the government assessed penalties against firms who would employ workers who had participated in them. Thus: ". . . it was alleged that firms not affected by the strikes which took on workers who had taken part in them were made to pay a fine of 1,000 pesetas ($16.75) for the first time and 6,000 pesetas ($100.50) the second time, while if they did so a third time, they were closed down."[15] Here is a most effective strike-breaking technique: either the workers give up the strike or they and their families face starvation.

Perhaps most significant of all is the charge that the Spanish government tolerated tortures against some of the 1963 strikers. Thus: ". . . in this communication the ICFTU and the IFCTU give details of the ill-treatment and tortures alleged to have been inflicted on Rafael Gonzáles, Silvino Zapico and his wife, Vicente Marañaga, Alfonso Braña and his wife, Antonio Zapico, Jeronimo Fernández Terente, Jesús Ramos Talavera, Everado Castro, Tino Martínez, Juan Alberdi and others. The first of those named was stated to have died as a result of his torture."[16] That such brutal action is not condoned by all the Spanish people is evidenced by the fact that the treatment of these strikers was protested in a letter signed by over 100 Spanish intellectuals. They addressed their letter to a Minister of Franco's cabinet. The ICFTU and the IFCTU managed to secure a copy of the letter and affixed it to its complaint to the ILO Committee on Free-

---

[13]Ibid., p. 61.

[14]Ibid., p. 61.

[15]Ibid., p. 64.

[16]Ibid., p. 64.

dom of Association.   The Spanish government denied that the strikers were tortured, conceding only that the head of one of the women prisoners was shaved.   Some groups in Spain and the complainants in the ILO requested that an international commission be sent to Spain to investigate the situation.   When the Spanish government refused to permit an investigation by such a commission, Spanish groups requested their government to allow an investigation by a commission composed only of Spanish attorneys and judges.   Even this request was refused by the Spanish government.   In view of this attitude, one can only conclude that the Spanish government does not want the world to learn of their treatment of striking Spanish workers.

RATIONALIZATION FOR STRIKE ILLEGALITY

As part of the rationalization for strike illegality, some Spanish writers argue that when strikes were lawful in the pre-Franco era, workers frequently lost them.   Hence, making them illegal did not really injure the workers' economic position.   In a review of strikes in Spain covering the period of 1905-1926, one study points out that there were a total of 4,324 strikes of which the author had information regarding the ultimate disposition. [17] Of this amount, the writer reports that workers won 1,073 strikes, lost 1,557, and 1,694 were settled by compromise.   He argues that such strike experience demonstrates the weakness of unions and the futility of strikes before the Franco regime was established.

If workers actually lost most strikes during the pre-Franco era, this may realistically be attributed to the lack of legal protection that Spanish unions and striking employees received from the state.   It is well known that U.S. labor organizations had great difficulties in the pre-Wagner Act era.   However, the direction of American labor policy was not to outlaw strikes but to shape a body of laws which makes more effective the opportunities of American workers to engage in successful collective action.

_____

[17] Jorge Arrufat, "Huelgas en España," Jornal, Órgano de Difusión Sindicalista, Organización Sindical Española, Servicio de Relaciones Exteriores, Madrid, No. 75, June-July, 1959, pp. 292-296.

If strikes are incompatible with Spain's current political structure and if the legalization of strikes and the protection of workers who engage in strikes would threaten the stability of the present government, it follows that strikes must be outlawed as a matter of self-preservation.   To outlaw strikes on this basis might be understandable under this premise and within this context.   However, to argue for the deprivation of the workers' right to strike--denying to them their only really effective weapon within a capitalistic society in which business is owned by individuals--on the grounds that they   generally lost strikes in prior years, is to beg the question of the moral and legal position of strikes within such an economic system.   In a capitalistic society such as Spain, where business is privately owned and where private employers are motivated by profits, the illegality of strikes appears to be incongruous.   This proposition has special significance in a nation where Catholicism is the official and state religion, because the Enciclica Rerum Noverum specifically mentions the strike as a moral right of workers in a capitalistic society.

RECOGNITION OF "COLLECTIVE CONFLICTS"

These theoretical conditions,   as well as the stubborn evidence of strikes during the Franco years, and particularly the bitter Asturias' strikes of 1962, induced the Spanish government to take a hard look at the Spanish workers' position. On September 20, 1962, the Ministry of Labor issued a decree which recognizes "collective conflicts."[18] This decree, regarded as revolutionary in some quarters in Spain, does not legalize any form of strike. Two leading Spanish authorities of labor law state in a commentary on this decree: ". . . there is not then recognition of its [the strike's] lawfulness, but it involves a certain degree of tolerance which reduces the mechanical application of penal punishment. . . ."[19] Before the enactment of the 1962 law, only individual disputes between

---

[18]Decreto del Ministerio de Trabajo, Número 2354, 20 Septiembre 1962. (Decree of the Ministry of Labor, Number 2354, September 20, 1962).

[19]G. Bayón Chacón and E. Pérez Botija, op. cit., p. 780.

an employer and employee were legally recognized under Spanish law. Special labor courts (<u>Magistratura</u> de <u>Trabajo</u>) were established to handle individual employee complaints against employers, such as individual dismissals and grievances involving failure to pay due wages, to award legal vacations and holidays, and to pay overtime rates, and other similar complaints. Collective complaints or conflicts did not have any standing under Spanish law, and the labor courts had no jurisdiction to handle them. Under the new decree, it is recognized that "abnormality in labor relations, as much in the individual as in the collective, although being an occasional situation, exceptional, limited, and transitory, is, nevertheless, a phenomenon with which law must reckon and regulate. In a developing economy, subject to processes of reorganization and technological change and governed by a desire of general elevation of the level of living of the people, a certain friction can develop, constituting a sign that labor relations do not remain immobile or stagnant, except that it is adapting to reality."

In other words, under the 1962 decree, Spanish workers lawfully may express to their employers a collective complaint, which, if not settled between them, may be heard by the Ministry of Labor. That body will attempt to resolve the dispute through conciliation. It also provides for conciliation through the Spanish Syndical Organization. If the dispute is not settled by conciliation, the Ministry of Labor may determine the outcome by compulsory arbitration, or may elect to submit the dispute to the Spanish special labor courts. The courts may either arbitrate the conflict or direct the parties to attempt to negotiate a collective bargaining contract. In practice, however, the Ministry of Labor has never submitted a dispute to the labor courts. Instead, it has either managed to effect a settlement through mediation or rendered a compulsory award. Actually, this fact is not too significant, since under Spanish law the special labor courts are under the jurisdiction of the Ministry of Labor, and in fact, the judges of these courts are appointed by the Ministry of Labor.

In short, the decree does not legalize the strike but instead provides a series of procedures to resolve a collective dispute between employers and employees. At the most, the decree recognizes that a strike could break out, and that penal sanctions will not be levied automatically against employees if they terminate the strike promptly and utilize the procedures that the decree makes available. That this is the limit of lawfulness of the strike is clearly expressed in the   1962 decree which states, in part, that "lack of observance of the procedures authorizes the employer to discharge the strikers." And, further, the government reserves to itself the "means that it estimates pertinent to guarantee the public order." That is, penalties can be applied under circumstances when the government believes them necessary to maintain the "public order." This obviously could be the case if the workers did not promptly terminate the strike and utilize the available procedures.

Furthermore, the language of the decree is such that Spanish workers risk danger any time they strike. It classifies collective disputes into (1) economic--those having a labor relations content and (2) political--those having as an objective a change in the political structure of the Franco regime. In the latter case, the appointed governors of the provinces or the central government are empowered to take whatever measures are necessary to break the strike, including the imposition of criminal penalties, the use of the military, and suspension of certain civil rights mentioned earlier.

The line that divides a political strike from an economic strike is indeed fine. Any strike could have both political and economic ends. A strike for higher wages may tend to breach a predetermined national wage policy. Is this, then, political or economic in character? Unfortunately, the decree of September 20, 1962 does not precisely define which collective conflict may be tolerated under its terms. Further, in any strike, it allows the classification of economic or political to be made by representatives of the Spanish government and not by any impartial, disinterested, or private forum.

In any event, the 1962 decree at least moves toward some liberalization for the Spanish worker. It is a step in the direction of a degree of self-determination for the Spanish laboring class. As one Spanish writer puts it: ". . . it does not mean that it has modified previous laws, since they continue the prohibition against conflicts [strikes] which alter national production or the economy or which have a political end, or which endanger the public order, etc., but . . . it establishes the possibility of a collective conflict which lawfully may take place, and constitutes a step in the progress of labor reality. It does not change the current rules, but it blends or tones down, though it is true not with desirable clarity, things."[20]

---

[20]José Alvarez de Miranda, op. cit., p. 173.

As this volume goes to press, there is some speculation that the Spanish government will legalize economic strikes or those engaged in for traditional trade union objectives.   During the summer of 1965 it is reported that the Labor Committee of the Spanish Cortes may recommend that strikes for trade union objectives be legalized. "Political" strikes will remain illegal. Thus, on June 28, 1965, the Christian Science Monitor states:

> Some of the harshness may be taken out of Spain's antistrike laws.   The Labor Committee of the Cortes (Parliament) is working in closed sessions on Article 222 of the Penal Code which defines strikes as punishable acts of sedition. A revised version is expected to be presented to the Cortes for approval when it meets this summer. A modified law would not legalize all strikes but it would distinguish between 'political' strikes and strikes motivated by economic and social discontent. Political strikes would still rank as seditious.

If the Spanish Parliament approves the new strike law in its present form, it is extremely doubtful that the concession will mean very much to Spanish workers. As stated, that line which divides political and economic strikes frequently cannot be drawn with precision. Furthermore, as long as the government makes the distinction between political and economic strikes, Spanish workers will be uncertain as to the scope of legal strike activity. At any time during the course of a strike, the government can brand a strike as political in character and oppressive measures can be undertaken to break the strike. This would be particularly true of strikes conducted on a broad industrial front. Such strikes could threaten the stability of the Franco government, and it is to expect much that the Spanish authorities will stand by and permit important strikes of this kind to continue for any length of time.

REGLAMENTACIONES:
THE SYSTEM OF MINIMUM LABOR LAWS

When it made the move to outlaw strikes, the Franco regime put itself in a position of responsibility to the Spanish workers.   José Antonio, in his blueprint for Spanish society, had promised the workers social justice under the new state.

In this society the interest of employers and employees were
to be balanced. Hence, from its beginning, the Franco regime adopted a policy of responsibility for establishing minimum labor standards.

Accordingly, the Rights of Labor stated that "work constitutes one of the most noble attributes of hierarchy and hon-
or and demands the assistance and protection of the State.
The State commits itself to exercise a constant and effective
action in the defense of the worker, his life and work." It
was, therefore, the state, and not collective action on the
part of the workers, that would be the guardian of the conditions of work. Thus, "the State will fix bases for the regulation of labor and the State will establish relations between
workers and employers."[21] The power to fix conditions of
work was subsequently conferred upon the Ministry of Labor. [22]
Under a law promulgated in 1942 the Spanish government affirmed that the establishment of working conditions would be
the "private function of the Ministry of Labor without any possible delegation." Any standards issued by this Ministry
would be in the form of minimums. An employer, if he de-
sired, could improve upon these minimums, being motivated
by humanitarianism or by conditions in the labor market. Decrees would be established for various sectors of industry,
and might apply to the entire nation, a province, two or more
provinces, or smaller territorial districts or regions within
a province. Accordingly, the reglamentaciones have an in-
dustrial-territorial basis. If the regulations merely covered
the 28 syndical groupings within the Spanish economy, only
28 of them would be in force. Rather, in practice, the reglamentaciones cover particular segments of a major branch of
industry enclosed within one syndicate. For example, there
is a regulation, not only for the entire banking industry, but
a particular one for each segment of the industry--savings
banks, industrial banks, building and loan banks, private
banks, mortgage banks, the Bank of Spain, etc. Indeed, as
of 1964, about 200 separate regulations were in force. Once

---

[21]Fuero del Trabajo, Title IV. (Rights of Labor).

[22]Ley de La Jefatura del Estado, Por LaQue Se Estab-
lecen Normas Para Regular La Elaboración de Las Reglamentaciones de Trabajo, October 16, 1942. (Law of the Chief of
State, for the Establishment of Norms to Regulate the Standards of Labor).

established, a particular labor code will cover all companies and workers covered by the standard. Thus, a reglamenta-ción "shall extend to all establishments, facilities, factories . . . to all branches and activities whatever may be their importance, size, or volume. . . . "[23]

Although the Ministry of Labor has full power and authority to issue minimum labor standards, the 1942 law states that before issuing any such decree the Spanish Syndical Organization must be consulted. The syndicates have the role of consultation in this regard and not of executive action. The Ministry of Labor is also encouraged to solicit the advice of other ministers, who head the various departments of the Spanish government, when such advice and counsel is deemed to be fruitful. As for the application and enforcement of the reglamentaciones, this is the function of the Labor Inspector, located within the Ministry of Labor, and the special labor courts. Fines and other penalties can be assessed against employers who violate the terms of a labor standard.

AN ILLUSTRATIVE REGLAMENTACIÓN

The reglamentaciones cover practically every phase of working conditions. The character of a typical labor standard can be illustrated by the one establishing working conditions in the hat, headdress, and button industry.[24] The whole regulation contains 222 pages with about 500 words to the page. Its scope is national, although such decrees may cover a smaller territorial area. After establishing its national character, it details the various job classifications involved in the manufacture of the products.   The labor force is divided into six major categories--operators, utility personnel, two administrative categories, technical jobs, and miscellaneous --and each contains a detailed breakdown of specific jobs, each accompanied by a job description. For example, the operator classification contains about 100 subclassifications. The minimum wage for each subclassification is then estab-

---

[23]G. Bayón Chacón and E. Pérez Botija, op. cit., p. 175.

[24]Reglamentaciones Nacionales de Trabajo de Confec-ción, Vestido y Tocado, Botones, Garcia Enciso, Madrid,1964.

lished, as well as other items, including standards for employee probationary periods, promotions, premiums for night and Sunday work, special payments for Christmas and July 18 (the date upon which the Spanish Civil War started), bonuses for outstanding workers, work schedules and hours, automatic wage increases for years of service, extra compensation for overtime work, vacations and holidays, sick leave and compensation for workers who are unable to work because of sickness, transfers of employees from one branch of a company to another branch, discipline, safety and health, a special fund for widows and dependents of deceased workers, protection of job rights of employees called to military service, special regulations for work performed in the homes of the workers, and many other items. Failure to conform to this detailed and comprehensive regulation carries penalties for the employer, ranging from fines for infractions to removal of company officials from their jobs for serious breaches.

DEFECTS OF THE SYSTEM

      Obvious inequities in the system constituted a primary defect in the government's attempt to balance the interests of employees and employers. For the former, the established minimum wage frequently became the maximum, regardless of a firm's ability to pay higher wages; for the latter, the existence of marginal firms was often placed in jeopardy, because of inability to pay the minimum wage, however low.
      These observations demonstrate the essential shortcomings of the reglamentaciones system of labor relations. They are applied across-the-board regardless of particular economic circumstances of a company covered by their terms. In a word, they are inflexible legal dispositions which at times have little reference to the realities of economic life. On this point, there is a general consensus among Spanish labor authorities and observers of the nation's labor picture. In April, 1958, the National Delegate of the Spanish Syndical Organization pointed out that the reglamentaciones provide standards "which are the same for all . . . and are uniform for every company within an industry . . . . We want to break the uniformity of the minimum salary."[25] About the same time, a

---

[25]Juan Eugenio Blanco, Estudio de Los Convenios Col-

subsecretary of the Ministry of Labor characterized the "rigid system of the fixation of wages by the State . . . ."[26] The General Manager of a large Spanish company was of the same judgment. He declared that under the system of reglamentaciones, employers and employees could not adjust to the "particulars" of his firm's conditions.[27] Editorials in the Spanish daily press frequently refer to the inflexibility of the system. Thus, in editorial comment, Ya, a major Madrid daily, commented that "to return exclusively to the old reglamentaciones would be a regression. The system established principles, created institutions and provided formulas still effective today. But the reglamentaciones were a solution required by the circumstances. To the question, return to the reglamentaciones exclusively, we reply emphatically, 'no!'"[28]

The economic implications of the reglamentaciones system are readily apparent. In its comprehensive study of the Spanish economy, the report of the World Bank refers to the impact of the system on labor mobility, productivity, and general economic progress.[29] Within the straight-jacket of the reglamentaciones system, employers and employees alike are denied the maximum opportunity for optimum utilization of their resources in the terms of economic progress. As will be pointed out, the general recognition of the shortcomings of the system of reglamentaciones was a pertinent factor for the adoption of Spain's collective bargaining law. However, the advent of this law did not replace the system of reglamentaciones. It still is in force in Spain today, and there appears to be no serious thought in Spanish government cir-

---

ectivos, Ministerio de Trabajo, Instituto Nacional de Previsión, Madrid, 1963, p. 25.

[26]Jornal, Organo de Difusión Sindicalista, Organización Sindical Española, Servicio de Relaciones Exteriores, Madrid, No. 67, March, 1958, p. 253.

[27]Problemas de Personal, Acción Social Patronal, Madrid, 1960, p. 164.

[28]Ya (Madrid), November 1, 1964.

[29]The Economic Development of Spain, International Bank for Reconstruction and Development, Baltimore: Johns Hopkins Press,   1963, p. 34.

cles to abolish the system. The system of legally imposed minimum labor standards remains one of the most important elements of Spain's labor relations system, and will probably continue to exist together with collective bargaining. Another development, supported by some syndicate and Ministry of Labor officials, might be to "codify" current reglamentaciones into a general labor code. Regardless of the changes that may be made in the system of reglamentaciones, the state will continue to fix minimum labor standards.

The foregoing commentary points up the salient features of the Spanish labor relations system prior to 1958. Independent labor unions and employer associations were abolished, and in their place the law created the Spanish Syndical Organization, embracing practically all employers and employees. Membership in the syndicate system was compulsory for all employers and employees subject to the jurisdiction of the organization. Strikes were declared unlawful, and employees engaging in strikes risked the possibility of penal sanctions. Minimum labor standards that frequently become the maximum standards were established by the state through the Ministry of Labor. Each firm of more than 50 workers was required to submit for state approval a code of working conditions.

This was the state of affairs when on April 24, 1958, the Spanish government for the first time under the Franco regime provided for a system of collective bargaining. Although analysis of the law will show that the state still plays an important role in the bargaining system, the legislation marks a major shift from the former policy of strict government control of labor relations. It must be noted that the current Spanish system of collective bargaining does not measure up to the kind of collective bargaining that exists in other Western nations; for example, the law does not permit utilization of economic weapons--the strike, lockout, picketing, and boycotts--to achieve collective bargaining contracts. Still, the present system does provide a measure of self-determination for both workers and employers in the labor relations area. It constitutes an important element in the wave of liberalization currently in vogue in Spanish society.

MOTIVATIONS FOR ENACTMENT

The 1958 law itself provides few clues to assess the factors that led to its enactment. True, its first article establishes that the new system was designed to promote the "spirit of social justice; facilitate the sense of unity of production and the community of labor; improve the standard of living of workers; and increase productivity." These declarations, however, are objectives of the legislation rather than the motivating factors for its passage. What then are some forces that resulted in the enactment of Spain's collective bargaining law?

Fundamental to this inquiry is the fact that before 1958, Spain was one of the few capitalistic societies that denied employees the right to negotiate collective bargaining contracts; for this reason, its labor program did not conform to the standards of the International Labor Organization. Added to this fact was the criticism by foreign labor unions and other labor bodies that the labor program of Spain did not conform to the doctrines of the Western world. It will be demonstrated that the Spanish collective bargaining system still fails to measure up to the standards of the ILO and that aspects of its labor relations system are still criticized by Western labor organizations.

Indeed, on March 1, 1965, the Executive Council of the AFL-CIO criticized the Franco system of labor relations. Its declaration, styled "Support the Fight for Freedom in Spain, " stated:

> The free trade unions of every country should reject unconditionally all moves of the (Spanish) Falangist union leaders to establish contacts with them. Such Falangist efforts have only one aim--to give the Spanish workers, who are denied trade union rights and all other democratic freedoms, the impression that the workers of the democratic countries now accept Franco 'unions' as bona fide labor organizations and recognize their officials as genuine spokesmen of the laboring people of Spain. We welcome the International Confederation of Free Trade Union's effort to have the free unions of the Common Market continue to bring maximum pressure for preventing the admission of Franco Spain into the European Economic Community or any agency thereof.

In any event, the 1958 law was an attempt by the Spanish government to make its nation more acceptable to the West. This volume stressed earlier that Spain's current political and economic structure depends largely upon its social, political, and economic integration and acceptance by the West. Such considerations undoubtedly played an important part in the enactment of the 1958 legislation, even though it is difficult to find in Spain written evidence of this.

The inflexible system of state-imposed labor standards proved to be an important hindrance to the productivity. As the years rolled on, and as Spain tried to increase productivity and raise its standard of living, the shortcomings of the state system of reglamentaciones became more and more evident. Clearly, it was necessary to adapt working conditions to the facts of economic reality on the plant level. A collective bargaining system was designed to provide the flexibility that was absent under the iron-clad, uniform system of state-established working conditions. A factor that contributed to the passage of the 1958 law, therefore, was recognition that productivity could be promoted by a more flexible and realistic system of establishing labor conditions. On this basis the World Bank study observed that "the widespread use of collective bargaining agreements is a recent development in the right direction."[1] The Spanish Syndical Organization characterizes the collective bargaining system as constituting a measure "to adapt to realistic conditions of the firm and industry, breaking the old uniformity of the reglamentaciones."[2] Also of significance is the declaration of a student of Spanish labor relations that the uniformity of the codes "produced negative effects in the area of wages--more graphically--the tendency to a low level of wages."[3] When minimum standards of wages become in practice maximum standards the consequences to worker productivity are obvious.

It is not surprising that many Spanish employers were not enthusiastic about the idea of establishing wages through collective bargaining. Thus, "some employers [still] believe that the state should continue to fix wages by legal decree.

---

[1]The Economic Development of Spain, International Bank for Reconstruction and Development, Johns Hopkins Press, Baltimore, 1963, p. 34.

[2]Tiempo Nuevo, Madrid, V. 10, No. 121, May, 1964, p. 72.

[3]Héctor Maravall, "Las Negociaciones Colectivas," Revista de Política Social, Instituto Estudios Políticos, Madrid, V. 57, 1963, p. 45.

These employers continue to believe that the state has the duty to fix by law minimum salaries."[4] In short, Spanish employers felt more comfortable under the system of reglamentaciones. Minimum wages often were established at very low
levels and this apparently suited at least the short-run interests of Spanish business. Significant in this respect was the
declaration of the official who was then Secretary General of
the technical branch of the Ministry of Labor. He stated that
factors causing the passage of the law were: "the perfection
and the growth of production; industrial expansion; the better
political and commercial position of Spain in the family of nations; and Spain's plan for economic development."[5]

Another contributing factor was the Spanish Syndical Organization's position in the area of labor relations. It has
been noted that the syndical system does not possess any executive power in the determination of Spanish working conditions; its role was limited to making recommendations to the
Ministry of Labor concerning reglamentaciones. As such, the
syndicate organization, despite its connection to the Spanish
state and despite its universality of membership, played a
secondary role in the establishment of working conditions. It
sought a more important function to aggrandize its role in the
critical area of labor relations. Hence, the plan to carry out
the collective bargaining system within the network of the
Spanish Syndical Organization would definitely suit its purposes. Success in this area would increase its general prestige and attractiveness to workers and employers. And it is
important to mention that in the network of competing governmental bureaucracies, the leaders of the Spanish Syndical Organization would correspondingly become more significant on
the political scene. It would not be fair, however, to conclude
that the syndical leaders supported a system of collective a-
greements merely to enhance their political position. It is
possible that they, as did other Spaniards, sincerely believed
that a system of collective bargaining agreements would be in
Spain's best interest.

In any event, the Syndical Organization early pressed
for a system of collective bargaining. As early as 1946 it ad-

---

[4]Ibid., p. 47.

[5]Francisco Norte, "Convenios Colectivos Sindicales,"
Revista de Trabajo, Ministerio de Trabajo, Madrid, V. 10,
October, 1958, p. 25.

vocated a system of collective agreements. [6] Despite this early support, under the present legislation the organization still plays a secondary role. Although agreements are negotiated within the Syndical Organization, the Ministry of Labor has the power to ratify or disapprove them. In short, the Syndical Organization still does not have executive power within the collective bargaining system. That this is resented by some syndical leaders at the present time is shown by their desire to divest the Ministry of Labor of this power.

Such then were the major motivating forces that led to enactment of Spain's 1958 collective bargaining law. Other factors may have been involved, such as the nation's hopes for better working conditions of employees, more equal distribution of the national income, and the development of a more responsible labor force. Another factor may be the criticism by some Spanish Catholic Church officials who viewed the pre-1958 strikes as evidence of workers' deep dissatisfaction with the labor relations program, and the development of some system of industrial "democracy" within the plant. However, these appear to be subsidiary rather than primary factors.

COLLECTIVE BARGAINING WITHIN
THE SYNDICAL NETWORK

Turning now to an analysis of the provisions and operation of the 1958 law, we are concerned primarily with the broad sweep of public policy rather than the minutiae of detail which would surround any law of magnitude. [7]

---

[6] I Congreso Nacional de Trabajadores, Delegación Nacional de Sindicatos, 1946, p. 85. The report of this conference states: "Labor norms which regulate (labor) activities should be proposed through the Syndical Organization by virtue of agreements of the representatives of employers and workers, reserving to the Ministry of Labor the ratification of the same."

[7] Also, on this point we shall not cite particular articles, sections, and paragraphs of the law. The basic law was approved on April 24, 1958, by the Spanish Parliament. One provision of the law authorizes the Ministry of Labor to "dictate necessary regulations to implement the present law." Subsequently, on July 22, 1958, the Ministry of Labor handed

The 1958 law requires that collective agreements be negotiated only within the network of the Spanish Syndical Organization. In fact, its actual title is "Ley de Convenios Colectivos Sindicales", or "Syndical Collective Agreements Law". On this point a Spanish labor authority states: ". . . our law adds the qualification 'syndical'. Our agreements are syndical because their negotiation is within the Syndical Organization . . . ."[8] To make the position absolutely clear, a former Minister of Labor stated in his analysis of the law before the Spanish Parliament: ". . . the life of the law is in the hands of the Spanish Syndical Organization."[9]

This condition is ensured by many features of the legislation. For example, those who actually negotiate the agreements previously have been chosen by employees and employers as syndical representatives. Thus, "the law does not provide for the choosing of specific representatives to negotiate labor agreements. The representatives chosen by the economic and social sections are those who are authorized to negotiate agreements. This is a job which they exercise as part of their duties."[10] Only those so chosen are authorized to institute negotiations and are empowered to ratify contracts after agreement. The contract does not depend on employers or employees, but only on acceptance by their syndical repre-

---

down a lengthy order to implement the provisions of the law. This is usual practice in Spain. Thus, after a law is approved by the Spanish Parliament, the law confers upon the appropriate ministry the power to implement its terms. The orders or regulations of a ministry have the power of law. Though such decrees cannot conflict with the basic law itself, the ministries have rather wide discretion in the application of a law. Observations as to substance of the 1958 law, of necessity, are based not only on the law itself but on the July 22, 1958, regulation of the Ministry of Labor and other rules which were handed down after this date.

[8]José Pérez Leñero, Convenios Colectivos Sindicales: Doctrina y Legislación, Madrid, 1959, p. 120.

[9]Convenios Colectivos Sindicales, Ministerio de Trabajo, Secretaria General Técnica, Madrid, 1958, p. 16.

[10]José Pérez Leñero, op. cit., p. 16.

sentatives. These considerations show that syndical elections should permit full freedom of selection, because any tampering with the election process can obviously impair the position of workers and employers in collective bargaining.

It is true that syndical organizations, or more accurately, the employer and the worker sections, may furnish advisors to help the elected representatives in the process of negotiation. Still, the action of accepting an agreement lies in the hands of the elected representatives. Employers may, and frequently do, hire independent consultants, usually attorneys, to aid them in the negotiations, in addition to the advisors made available through the syndical system. On the other hand, lack of money usually prevents the workers' groups from hiring outside help. This tips the scales in favor of the employers, and tends to underscore the commonly held judgment that employers play the more powerful role in the Spanish Syndical Organization. [11] In this context, an editorial in a Spanish daily newspaper comments: ". . . much friction has been produced in the negotiations because of lack of preparation of the workers before negotiations."[12] This "lack of preparation" of the workers probably reflects the poor quality of their advisors.

A negotiation may not begin without the approval of an appointed official of a syndical organization. If a proposed contract is limited to one province, approval must be by the syndical delegate of that province; an interprovincial agreement requires approval by the president of a syndicate. In order to obtain approval, the employer and employee representatives must send to the appropriate syndical authority an agenda of the major points of negotiation. This practice allows the appointed syndical officials to postpone or prevent the start of negotiations, thus affording them effective veto power over elected officials.

Yet another authority has indicated a desire to possess veto power in this context. Some factions of the Ministry of Labor believe that this body should have this power over the Syndical Organization, [13] thus revealing another area of the

---

[11]New York Times, (American Edition), October 28, 1964.

[12]La Nueva España (Ovedio), September 14, 1964.

[13]See, for example, José Pérez Leñero, op. cit., p.

battle for power between the two organizations.

Though it has the power to veto the start of negotiations, actually the Spanish Syndical Organization has interfered very infrequently with the negotiation of agreements, and when it has, syndical officials have responded (as they must) to directives of the Spanish government. It is, of course, in the interest of the Spanish Syndical Organization to encourage the use of collective agreements, and to increase its prestige by successfully settling contracts. Still, the fact that it has a veto power over the start of negotiations is significant, as a potential barrier to the free will of Spanish employers and employees in the area of collective bargaining. Moreover, by the use of such power it can influence the direction, if not the total volume, of contracts. In contrast, no similar policy exists in the United States. In the United States, once a union represents a majority of workers in the bargaining unit, it may negotiate a contract. It needs no approval from any government or quasi-government agency.

An additional duty of the Spanish Syndical Organization is to establish the minutiae of detail surrounding the execution of the 1958 law, under a comprehensive code to regulate the negotiation of contracts and the general development of the law. [14] A detailed analysis of this regulation is beyond the scope of this volume, and, in fact, would add little to an understanding of the basic policies of Spanish collective bargaining. [15] The regulation, issued on July 23, 1958, is long

---

139, wherein the author, who is an official of the Ministry of Labor, states: ". . . we do not believe that the Ministry of Labor should be denied the final decision for the initiation of negotiations. . . ."

[14]Normas Sindicales de 23 de Julio de 1958 Para La Aplicación de La Ley Convenios Colectivos, Boletín de La Organización Sindical de 9 de Septiembre de 1958. (Sindical Norms of July 23, 1958 for the Application of the Collective Agreement Law, Bulletin of the Sindical Organization of September 9, 1958).

[15]For example, the syndicate regulation establishes which syndical group has the authority to represent employers and employees in a particular negotiation, details the specific procedure to request permission to start negotiations, and deals with the selection of the "President" of a negotiation and

and comprehensive, covering about 14 printed pages, and, in fact, is about twice as long as the law itself.   One point is of significance in this respect.   Once again the Spanish government demonstrates little faith in the elected employer and employee representatives to adopt collective procedures of their own choosing. The syndically imposed rules of procedure introduce an element of inflexibility in the negotiations that tends to inhibit innovations and the imagination of the direct participants.   In short, collective bargaining procedures are established for them, as well as a framework within which they must strive to find solutions.

The power of the Spanish Syndical Organization to lay down the details for use of the law should not be confused with the authority to establish conditions of employment when the parties fail to agree at the bargaining table.   This power is lodged exclusively in the Ministry of Labor.

THE SCOPE OF THE BARGAINING UNIT

The Spanish collective bargaining law deals with the scope of the bargaining unit.   Contracts may cover one of a wide variety of bargaining units: one company or a group of companies within a city, county, or province; or a single firm or different companies that operate in two or more provinces. The latter bargaining unit is referred to as "interprovincial." What kind of unit will be covered by an agreement will depend on what syndical group initiates the negotiation.   Ordinarily, that is the worker section, though in a few cases a company or

---

his powers. (Under the 1958 law the syndicates are empowered to appoint the so-called President of the negotiations. Thus, the parties are not free to choose such a President or to negotiate without any officially designated chairman. The powers of the President of a Spanish collective bargaining negotiation include a variety of subjects, the most important one being his authority to serve as a conciliator if the parties are unable to agree by themselves.) It also establishes how many people may represent the respective parties in negotiations, the system for the appointment of syndical advisors, rules that govern the contractual negotiations, and conditions under which a negotiation may be suspended because of the impossibility of reaching an agreement or because of evidence that one of the

a group of employers takes the initiative. For example, a medium size clothing company that did this stated that "one of the advantages of the law is to provide the company the initiative to depart from the system of official fixation [i.e., the system of reglamentaciones] and general character of salaries and working conditions which did not take into account the characteristics of each firm . . . ."16

An important restriction of the law is this: negotiation may not begin unless a contract when consummated would cover a company or a group of companies that have at least 100 workers. Originally, this figure was placed at 500, but in 1959 the Ministry of Labor lowered the figure to 100, as more realistic in view of the size of typical Spanish firms. In 1964, about 80 per cent of the Spanish industrial firms employed less than 10 workers, [17] and the typical firm is small, employing few workers. Many Spanish firms employ hundreds and even thousands of workers, so that most firms are either very small or relatively large. As an aside it may be remarked that if Spain is to improve its productivity significantly it would follow that the small size firm must fall by the wayside. Recent efforts of the Spanish government to facilitate the merger of small firms into larger units as yet have not proved successful. Hence, the more realistic figure of 100 permitted the broader implementation of the collective bargaining law.

One major problem is involved in the bargaining unit structure of the Spanish collective bargaining system. Agreements will typically cover more than one company in a particular branch of industry. Thus, of the 3,532 agreements in force as of June 30, 1964, the Spanish Syndical Organization reports that only 923 were negotiated on a company basis. The

---

parties exhibited bad faith or fraud.

[16]Problemas de Personal, Acción Social Patronal, Madrid, 1960, p. 149. See also Javier M. de Bedoya, "La Experiencia Española de Los Convenios Colectivos", Cuadernos de Previsión Laboral, No. 18, 1963, p. 44. On this point the writer states: ". . . for many years, all the applications for agreements came from the workers, but lately, for agreements which will cover different employers, the initiative has come from the employers because of competitive factors."

[17]Hoja del Lunes (Madrid), October 5, 1964.

remainder covered two or more firms. This means that frequently a single negotiation will cover plants of different economic characteristics. A man who has presided at many collective bargaining negotiations observed that in one negotiation "there may be different firms of unlike technology, some which are highly mechanized and other plants where hand labor predominates."[18] For example, the same negotiation involved two large factories and another company that operated various small shops. "The two big factories were represented by two representatives and the smaller operation by only one." This situation provided an unfair advantage to the larger firms, which sought an agreement to fit their needs to the disadvantage of the smaller company. Such a procedure, he observed, could result in a situation which could "sweep away one or more competitors." On the other hand, grouping together in a single negotiation companies in different stages of economic development, technological characteristics, locations, and market conditions could result in disadvantages to the workers. Under such diverse circumstances, the terms of the agreement could tend to seek their lowest level. Thus, such negotiations "are generally used by companies to arrive at a salary level based upon the conditions of the firms" which have the least ability to pay.[19]

Seeking a solution to this bargaining unit problem, the Minister of Labor has begun to encourage the negotiation of single-company collective bargaining contracts. This is not a practical solution because of the typical small size of firms in Spain. A more satisfactory solution may be to encourage bargaining units that would differentiate companies by size of labor force. That is, for the same branch of industry, firms could be ranked on the basis of small, medium, and large companies. For a particular territorial area and industrial branch, contracts would cover firms depending upon the size of the establishments. But even this proposal has important defects; for example, it would tend to hinder the growth of small firms. Nevertheless it appears more sensible than the present situation whereby a single negotiation covers plants and shops of significantly different economic characteristics.

---

[18]Javier M. de Bedoya, op. cit., p. 46.

[19]Emilio Torres Callego, "El Diálogo en El Mundo del Trabajo," Cuadernos Para El Diálogo, Madrid, No. 10-11, July-August, 1964, p. 11.

CONTENT OF THE AGREEMENTS

One provision of the law establishes the issues that can be resolved in collective agreements. The language of this feature of the law is such that practically all areas of labor relations can be included in a contract. The exceptions to this proposition involve peculiar features of Spanish labor relations law--a subject which will be subsequently treated. Items that may be included in collective bargaining agreements are: wages; incentive systems of payment; job classification; promotions; adaptation to changes in new working methods or technology; reduction in hours (but without reduction in productivity); revision of work schedules; compensation for sickness or accidents; safety systems; welfare and health; profit sharing programs; holidays and vacations; and worker training and educational systems. Also, by a decree issued by the Minister of Labor in 1959 an agreement may include provisions that supplement and improve on the state system of social security.

Unfortunately, it is beyond the scope of this study to make a systematic comparative analysis of the provisions of Spanish labor agreements. As of September, 1964, there were in existence 4,532 contracts. A meaningful analysis of the content of the agreements would obviously require a study by itself. Though Spanish literature on collective agreements is plentiful, and despite the requirement in the Spanish collective bargaining law that all agreements must be published in their entirety in official government bulletins, the literature apparently lacks studies that present a comparative analysis of the agreements' contents.

On the basis of the reading of scores of agreements, however, it can be concluded that Spanish agreements usually deal with almost all the subjects covered by the law. As expected, the larger firms provide better benefits than the smaller companies, and there is some tendency in the larger companies to negotiate systems of profit sharing and wage incentives. Considering the comparatively low level of Spanish wages and productivity, such systems are wholesome and in the interest of all parties. This study will attempt to provide at least the flavor and the tendencies of the Spanish labor agreements.

Some contracts exhibit provisions based on the social, economic, and cultural heritage of Spanish society. One problem of some Spanish firms is poor attendance and punctuality of workers. This has given rise to contractual provisions for a bonus to workers who are regular in attendance and who report to work on time. These bonuses are quite small--about seven cents per day--but they are large enough to serve the purpose and they are not an unimportant fringe benefit. Other provisions pertain to the customary Spanish working day. Many firms operate on a schedule that includes a long "lunch period" of about two to three hours, operating from 8 AM to 1 PM, shutting down until 4 PM, and resuming at that time until 7 PM. Convention tends to impair the most effective operation of the firm. Although one would expect Spanish workers to oppose this schedule because it interferes with family and recreational activities, the fact is that Spanish society stubbornly clings to the system and the habit is not easily broken. Accordingly, the continuous eight hour day, accepted by the Western world as normal, at times becomes an issue for negotiation. That there is some tendency to adopt the continuous eight hour day is noted in some agreements covering the larger plants, particularly in firms owned in part by foreign companies. For example, with respect to a Chrysler operated automobile plant, it is stated that the facility "operates on the relatively innovational schedule of 7 AM to 3 PM with time off for 'sandwich' breaks only."[20]

Some provisions are oriented to the comparatively paternalistic character of Spanish society and to its low wage structure. For example, one contract provides that the company will pay some of the school expenses of their workers' children; award a baby bed and layette for newly born children; provide upon request the equipment for the first communion; advance wages to workers who desire to buy furniture for their houses; provide a dowry for all female employees upon marriage, equivalent to a month's salary for each year of service, up to six; and give employment to children of workers.[21] Educational aid to children is not an unimportant consideration. Of each 100 students enrolled in the University of Madrid only one is the child of a worker while 67 are children of business-

[20]Spain's American Weekly, Madrid: Guidepost Publications, November 6, 1964, p. 17.

[21]"Magnífico Sentido Social de Un Convenio Colectivo." Revista de Legislación Social, No. 221, March 1962, pp. 69-72.

men or professional persons. [22]

A good share of Spanish collective agreements deal with housing of employees. Despite the fact that the Spanish government has made an effort to remedy the housing situation, adequate housing that workers can afford is in extremely short supply. Accordingly, some of the larger Spanish firms have housing units available for their workers, and the right to use such housing is negotiated in some Spanish agreements. [23]

Despite a recent trend of industrialization, Spain remains essentially an agricultural society. In 1960, 42 per cent of the Spanish labor force was engaged in agriculture. [24] Obviously, many labor agreements are in the agricultural area. As of September, 1964, of the 4,532 collective agreements in force within the nation, 2,009 covered agricultural establishments and 2,000 applied to industrial firms, and only 523 covered service establishments. [25] Characteristics of the agricultural agreements correspond in general with those negotiated in industry and services, although some features are uniquely related to agricultural pursuits. One study of agricultural agreements reports that they provide for: increases of wages above those established by law; bonuses depending upon employee output; improvement in hours of work; regulation of rest periods; payment of a small travel allowance for workers from their homes to their places of employment; premiums for work performed on Sundays and holidays; reduction of the minimum number of days required to earn vacation benefits; and July 18 (national holiday) and Christmas bonuses that correspond at times to those enjoyed by workers

---

[22]Ya (Madrid), November 20, 1964.

[23]Problemas de Personal, op. cit., p. 76.

[24]Anuario Estadístico de España, Presidencia del Gobierno, Instituto Nacional de Estadística, Madrid, 1963, and 1964, p. 49.

[25]"Estadística General de Los Convenios Sindicales Desde La Promulgación de La Ley (1958) Hasta El 30 de Junio de 1964," Vicesecretaria Nacional de Ordenación Social, Organización Sindical Española, p. 1.

in industry and service occupations.[26] Another study of outstanding features of agricultural labor agreements points out
that they provide: an automatic wage increase every three
years instead of every five, which is common in the system of
reglamentaciones; payments for work beyond the standard
eight-hour day; leaves of absence; special benefits for sickness
or injury; and a system of production standards and bonuses
according to specific tasks.[27]

CONTRASTS WITH UNITED STATES CONTRACTS

Greater understanding of the Spanish collective bargaining system and the content of the agreements may be gained
by studying some outstanding contrasts between contracts in
Spain and in the United States. These differences are explained
in terms of the peculiarities of the system of Spanish industrial relations law, particularly with respect to the application and the enforcement of Spanish agreements, as no system
of private arbitration is provided under the law. Some agreements provide for an internal grievance procedure to handle
employee complaints. For example, in a contract that applies
to a large metallurgical company, a grievance procedure is
established. A worker grievance is defined as a "manifesta-
tion of displeasure by the worker for acts which affect his dig-
nity, his work, and human relations between the personnel of
the Company and the work force." A worker is authorized to
present his claim orally by himself or through his syndical
representative to his immediate supervisor, who then has two
days to resolve the complaint. If it is not settled within two
days, the worker may submit his complaint in writing to the
company's personnel department, which will attempt to settle
the claim within four days. If he is still unsatisfied, the worker is then authorized to submit his dispute to the labor-man-

---

[26]"Los Convenios Colectivos Sindicales de Trabajo en
Las Actividades Agropecurias," Jornal, Madrid, No. 80,
April-May, 1960, p. 236.

[27]Los Convenios Colectivos Sindicales en El Sector
Agrario, Organización Sindical Española, Servicio de Información y Publicaciones Sindicales, Madrid, 1962, pp. 11-13.

agement committee, and then to the plant manager. [28]

So far, the procedure reflects similarity to American collective bargaining contracts. The great difference occurs when, if the worker is not satisfied with the plant manager's decision, he or his representatives cannot invoke private arbitration. If the complaint involved a disagreement over the application or the interpretation of a provision in the agreement, the dispute will be determined by representatives of the Ministry of Labor. Thus, the law provides that the "labor authority which approved the agreement shall be authorized to resolve any doubts as to its meaning, significance, or scope," and the Spanish government, not private arbitrators, will resolve disputes regarding the meaning and application of contractual language.

If the complaint involves an alleged company violation of an agreement which affects him personally, such as failure to pay the stipulated wages or to provide him with contractually established vacation or holiday benefits, or any other of the variety of complaints that have an individual worker orientation, and if the alleged company violation cannot be settled at the plant level, special government labor courts may ultimately settle the dispute. The Spanish collective bargaining law outlines the procedure to be followed in the event of a claim that the company violated a contract under these circumstances. The worker's representative contacts a representative of the Labor Inspector's office, which is under the jurisdiction of the Ministry of Labor. It is the duty of the Labor Inspector's office to assure employer compliance with all of Spain's labor laws, such as social security, minimum wages, safety and health, and child and women labor, as well as to assure compliance by employers with the terms of collective bargaining agreements. In the first quarter of 1964, there were 400 labor inspectors who discovered 1,201 violations of collective bargaining agreements. These violations are referred to the special labor court which is authorized to affix money penalties against the errant employers and to require them to make good any monetary losses suffered by employees because of employer violations.

Spanish labor agreements do not provide for an internal system to resolve in a final and binding manner disputes with respect to discharge or discipline of employees for cause. The reason for this is that the Spanish labor courts have final

---

[28] Problemas de Personal, op. cit., p. 157.

jurisdiction over such disputes. [29] To put it in other terms, Spanish employers do not have the unilateral right to discipline employees. Any employee who is discharged may appeal the employer's decision to the labor courts. The advent of the Spanish collective bargaining law did not change this longstanding and fundamental feature of Spanish labor relations law. Consequently, the final determination of discharge disputes is not a subject of collective bargaining.

To be sure, many agreements establish the reasons for discipline, and such reasons are comparable with those that are in effect in any system of company labor relations--excessive absenteeism, tardiness, deliberate stalling on the job, gross insubordination, failure to use safety equipment, intoxication, and the like; these company rules must not conflict with those that are established under Spanish law. Also, some agreements provide an internal grievance procedure wherein the employee may challenge the decision of the employer. However, as would be true in the case of the absence of a labor agreement, an employee who refuses to accept the final judgment of the employer may carry his case to the labor courts.

Under the system established by the reglamentaciones, the following discharge procedure is in force. The employer must state the cause of the discharge in writing, and such notice must contain the date of the action. As stated, discharge may reflect only a cause that has been established by the Ministry of Labor. An employee has 15 days to protest the discharge to the labor courts. However, before the judge may take jurisdiction of the case, an appropriate syndical official must attempt to conciliate the dispute. Before handing down an award, the labor courts also must attempt to mediate the dispute. If the discharge is declared to be unjust by the court, the employer may be required either to reinstate the worker in his former job, or to indemnify the employee in an amount fixed by the court up to one year's salary. If the employer has less than 50 workers, he may choose one of the above alternatives; if the employer has more than 50 workers, the choice is made by the employee. In proceedings before the labor courts, the employee may obtain without charge the services of an attorney furnished by the Spanish Syndical Organization. The worker is free to retain private counsel, but in

_____

[29]Decreto del Ministerio de Trabajo, 26 Enero 1944. (Decree of the Ministry of Labor, January 26, 1944).

that case he would be required to pay the attorney's fee. Because of low wages, the worker usually accepts the attorney supplied by the syndical system.

Unfortunately, statistics are not available that precisely define the experience of the labor courts in the matter of discharge. Figures available are to show the disposition of all cases that have been decided by the courts regardless of their content, including cases involving an employer's failure to pay legal wages or to conform to any other labor benefits conferred upon workers by a reglamentación, such as vacations, holidays, promotions, overtime compensation, and the like. Also, the statistics include any judgment by the labor courts involving the worker's charge of violation of a labor agreement. Thus, the following statistics reflect the experience of all cases, regardless of content, decided by the Spanish labor courts for 1959 through 1963. [30]

Effect on the Worker	1959	1960	1961	1962	1963
Favorable	9,673	9,840	8,743	8,734	10,985
Unfavorable	9,261	9,257	8,414	6,954	7,582
Partly Favorable	3,097	3,691	2,232	4,312	4,346

In recent years there has been considerable agitation to permit employers the right to discharge without court review. It is argued that the Spanish employer "has about lost the authority of management and that we do see, therefore, another solution to remedy the dangerous position of our domestic economy and our international markets."[31] The implication of such an argument, of course, is that court review of the disciplinary powers of management considerably impairs the nation's productivity, and that a system of free discharge would allow plants to operate more effectively with the result of attracting "more foreign capital into Spain."

This view, however, is not shared by Spanish authorities, whose opinion is represented by an editorial in a leading Madrid daily, which states: "we have opposed repeatedly

---

[30]Anuario Estadístico de España, op. cit., p. 253.

[31]Manuel Izquierdo, "Despidos Libres," Revista de Legislación Social, Madrid, No. 192, October, 1959, p. 299.

the liberty of applying the maximum penalty without an effective defense of the workers against injustices."[32] But it is
the case that under a system that prohibits independent labor
unions and the right to strike, and in the absence of a legal
provision to permit private arbitration of discharge disputes,
Spanish workers are at the mercy of the employer. Accordingly, court review of discharge is a provision necessitated by
the over-all system of labor relations in force in Spain, and
would be necessary even if it might tend to impair productivity.

The observer is led to expect that the Spanish Syndical
Organization would favor a system of free discharge if the collective bargaining law were changed to provide for private
arbitration. This would lend more prestige to collective bargaining contracts and would tend to make worker membership
in the syndicates more meaningful, leading more workers to
seek collective bargaining agreements. On the contrary, the
syndical organization has consistently opposed free discharge.
On this point, the workers' section of a national syndicate
with a membership of 1 million workers manifested "its string-
ent protest against the proposals made in the press, radio, and
TV for a system of free discharge",[33] complaining that advocacy comes from representatives of management. This position demonstrates the syndicates lack of confidence in their
ability to provide employees with adequate protection against
unfair discharge. It rejects an opportunity to establish a policy which would substitute authentic trade union action for the
current system of state control of labor relations. One could
readily imagine the outburst of protest from the American labor movement to a proposal which would strip collective bargaining of its capacity to protect workers from unjust discharge
and in its place substitute a system of labor courts!

Another very important difference that distinguishes
Spanish agreements from those of the United State is their
lack of provision for the protection of workers against layoff
because of economic conditions, including technological change.
As in the case with discharge for cause, employers do not
have the power to lay off workers because of economic conditions without governmental intervention, but must obtain approval from the Ministry of Labor. The employer must sub-

---

[32]Ya (Madrid), November 6, 1964.

[33]Ya (Madrid), November 24, 1964.

mit a petition specifying the number of "permanent" workers he desires to lay off and his reasons. Within 30 days, the Ministry of Labor will decide not only how many, but also which workers may be laid off.

In executing its authority to regulate layoffs, the Ministry of Labor applies a number of standards, including such items as the economic position of the firm, the state of its economic development, the efficiency of workers and their disciplinary record, and the number of dependents of the workers. Governmental control of this vital phase of management authority has important productivity implications despite whatever attention may be paid by the Ministry of Labor to the realities of economic life, because no one is better qualified than the employer to judge the labor force he needs to meet the economic circumstances of his firm. The current system discourages the installation of new equipment to improve efficiency. The possibility that the government will not sanction the layoff of employees who are no longer needed   inhibits the purchase of new machinery to replace manpower. The system also tends to discourage employers from seeking new markets that might require the expansion of the labor force. The development of new markets could result in the expansion of the firm, and to meet the new demand the employer in good faith might hire permanent employees or convert temporary employees to a permanent status. If the dynamics of the marketplace should subsequently result in the curtailment or the loss of the new markets, the employer might be faced with the possibility of retaining surplus labor. Thus, he is discouraged from seeking new markets in the first place.

Important economic considerations are recognized in this statement by the World Bank from its study on the Spanish economy:

> Under the existing regulations governing industrial employment, workers can be dismissed for 'economic' [as distinct from disciplinary] reasons only through a procedure involving the permission of the Ministry of Labor. In economic terms, this system must be considered as to the needs of the developing economy. Replacement of old and inefficient equipment may be inhibited to the extent that the gains from the use of new machinery are dissipated through the need to retain labor made superfluous by its introduction. Also, entrepreneurs may be hesitant to engage in new ventures

that involve an increase in their labor force if the force must be maintained in full even if it should later prove to be excessive. [34]

Frankly, government review of employers' decisions in the area of layoffs appears inconsistent with the objectives of Spain's unemployment compensation law, adopted in 1961. [35] Since Spanish workers may obtain unemployment compensation while laid off, it follows that employers should be permitted to adjust their labor force according to economic need without obtaining government approval. In general, the law provides unemployment compensation of 75 per cent of the basic wage, plus family allowance, for a period up to six months. At this writing (1964) Spain is in the first of its four year plans for economic development. [36] Nothing in the plan suggests that Spain intends to follow the suggestion implicit in the World Bank's observations, a recommendation that undoubtedly would do much for the development of the Spanish economy.

Other differences that distinguish Spanish labor agreements from those in force in the United States may be briefly noted. Because of the compulsory membership feature of the Spanish Syndical Organization, the agreements do not contain any union security arrangements. Of course there is a dramatic difference between union security arrangements found in American contracts and the "compulsory union" feature of Spain's syndical system. The latter requires membership through force of law while the former is negotiated by employers and unions on a private basis. No law in the United States forces any worker to join any union. Taft-Hartley legislation is merely permissive in this respect; the decision to negotiate a union security arrangement is the choice of the union and the employer. Clearly, in the light of Spanish experience, a law requiring membership in United States labor unions would con-

---

[34]The Economic Development of Spain, op. cit., p. 344.

[35]See "Ayudas Para Las Situaciones de Paro Por Reconversión de Industrias," Ministerio de Trabajo, Oficina de Divulgación, 1963, pp. 1-15 for a popular account of this law.

[36]Summary of the Spanish Economic and Social Development Plan, 1964-1967, Commission of the Government Development Plan, Office of Public Relations, Madrid, 1964.

stitute the antithesis to a free system of trade unionism. It is indeed significant that during World War II when the U.S. government through the National War Labor Board was empowered to decide any dispute which threatened the war effort, President Roosevelt was opposed to any decision by the NWLB that would force a worker to join a union. He reflected the heritage and the principles of a free society when he stated: "I tell you quite frankly that the Government of the United States will not order, nor will the Congress pass legislation ordering, a so-called closed shop."

Finally, there is obviously no need for the Spanish agreement to include "no strike" clauses. As a Spanish author puts it: "Since all kinds of strikes are illegal under our law, it is not necessary to cover them as do the authors of contracts in foreign nations."[37] Of course, under Spanish labor law, an employer may discharge workers for engaging in strikes or for engaging in a deliberate slow down; therefore, such a penalty need not be stated in labor agreements. Indeed, discharge is the mildest of penalties that may be imposed against striking Spanish employees.

AT THE BARGAINING TABLE

Several outstanding features dealing with the face-to-face negotiation of agreements shed additional light upon Spain's collective bargaining system. The 1958 law deals with the possibility that one or another of the parties may not appear at the negotiations authorized by a Spanish Syndical Organization official. Since the worker syndical sections normally take the initiative to petition for a contract, the penalty for nonappearance in practice relates to the employer's position if he deliberately refuses to attend a negotiation. In this case a syndical official advises the Ministry of Labor of the absence, and at the same time furnishes to the ministry a report covering the economic position of the firm and other pertinent data, including a list of the proposals of the worker group. The Ministry of Labor is then authorized by law to hand down an award, which, in effect, means writing the labor agreement.

Several considerations are involved in this feature of

37José Pérez Leñero, op. cit., p. 93.

the law.   Under the circumstances of nonappearance, and the subsequent award by the Ministry of Labor, there is, of course, no collective bargaining.   As a Spanish writer points out: "the imposition in this case has something of the character of discipline and lacks the cooperation of the absent party."[38]   Any collective bargaining law must, of course, take into consideration the possibility that one party or the other may refuse to negotiate.   The Spanish law can be challenged in that the government writes the contract under these circumstances; methods of dealing with this problem are available other than a state-dictated decree.   One alternative is imposition of a financial penalty; another is to force the reluctant party to the bargaining table.   The United States has chosen to force the employer to bargain collectively by a court injunction.   Failure to obey the injunction can result in money fines or imprisonment.   Such a procedure is more in keeping with the spirit and principles of collective bargaining than the present Spanish solution.

These same observations apply to the feature of the Spanish law that prevents bad faith, fraud, or coercion at the bargaining table.   Under the terms of the legislation, a negotiation can be suspended if the syndical organization finds either party guilty of such conduct.   Under these circumstances, the sanctions of the law can be twofold: if the party who requested negotiation engaged in bad faith, fraud, or coercion, it will not be permitted to request collective bargaining for six months.   If the other party engaged in such conduct, the Ministry of Labor is authorized to write the collective bargaining contract.   If the institution of collective bargaining is to be advanced, fines or penal sanctions can be assessed against the errant party.   In short, the burden of the negotiation of the contract should fall to the parties and not to the government.   Under the present scheme, there is no collective bargaining; in its place is a system that involves a government-dictated decree.

Experience has shown that collective bargaining sessions in Spain are at times prolonged, often because of stalling by employer representatives.   For example, in a letter to a Madrid daily newspaper a writer complains that "it took two years in order to reach an agreement in negotiations."[39]   In the Un-

---

[38]Ibid., p. 142.

[39]El Alcazar (Madrid), November 20, 1964.

ited States, such delaying action on the part of employers is not possible. The union either would seek relief under the terms of the Taft-Hartley law or strike. On the Spanish scene, however, workers may not strike, and nothing in Spanish law prohibits these delaying tactics at the bargaining table. As long as he appears to be negotiating and avoids a charge of bad faith, an employer can stall negotiations indefinitely.

An additional defect of negotiations involves sharing information at the bargaining table. Employers frequently refuse to divulge information involving their economic capacity to meet employee demands. Furthermore, economic data which is furnished to employee representatives is at times misleading if not completely false. It is said that in Spain employers prepare four financial statements--one for stockholders, one for tax purposes, one for collective bargaining purposes, and one for the controlling management and owners of the firm. Only the latter apparently accurately reflects the economic situation of the firm. That this is a real problem, producing friction at the bargaining table and making intelligent and rational negotiations difficult, is expressed in statements by high officials of the workers' section in the Spanish Syndical Organization.

Indeed, the refusal of some Spanish employers to provide relevant and accurate information at the bargaining table undoubtedly sparked the following bitter criticism:

> Unfortunately there are many employers who do not have a social sense. They do not concede importance to their relations with their workers. They discuss a collective agreement with the spirit, not of establishing a social policy accomodated to present and future needs, but with defending themselves, from what they consider as an attack to their property. And, therefore, it is necessary to recognize that communication is communication among the deaf . . . . [40]

It is well known that American employers are obligated to furnish relevant economic data in negotiations in which they plead inability to meet employees' demands. [41] A change in the

---

[40] Emilio Torres Gallego, op. cit., p. 12.

[41] N. L. R. B. v. Truit Manufacturing Company (1956),

Spanish law to adopt such a policy would represent a wholesome development, making collective bargaining negotiations more fruitful, intelligent, and rational.

By far, the most important and difficult issue in contemporary Spanish collective bargaining is wages, simply because of the low level of Spanish wages. On January 17, 1963, the Spanish government put into effect a minimum wage law in Spain amounting to $1.00 per day. Although only about 2 million Spanish workers, mostly in agriculture, were earning less than this, the low level of the Spanish minimum wage reflects the general wage structure.

The following chart demonstrates the pattern of Spanish wages for typical occupational groups in 1963. Though they increased substantially by 1963 and are undoubtedly higher at present, Spanish wage levels are among the very lowest in Europe, and, of course, would be considered as substandard by American standards. The chart reflects average hourly earnings, including all special compensation and bonuses. Also, it should be noted that the occupational classifications reflect comparatively skilled labor. Obviously, wages for unskilled labor would be correspondingly lower.

AVERAGE HOURLY EARNINGS
OF SPANISH WORKERS 1963*

Occupation	Hourly Earnings
Accounting Clerk	$ .72
Bank Office Clerk	.67
Bricklayer	.42
Carpenter	.36
Clerk Typist	.42
Coal Cutter	.67
Conductor	.42
Driver	.50
Electrician	.39
Insurance Office Clerk	.58
Knitting Machine Operator	.34
Mechanic (automobile)	.58
Painter (building)	.37
Pastry Maker (bakery)	.42

---

351 U. S. 149.

Occupation	Hourly Earnings
Plumber	$ .47
Private School Teacher	.67
Rolling Mill Operator (metal industry)	.44
Salesman in Retail Trade	.55
Shoe Maker (factory)	.32
Stereotyper	.50
Typographer	.34
Welder	.37

*Source: The wage data were computed on information supplied by the Spanish Syndical Organization, the National Institute of Statistics, and painstaking study of many 1963 collective bargaining contracts.

This writer had an opportunity to visit a Madrid plant that manufactures chairs. At the time of the visit, the factory employed 16 workers who operated modern machines in the fabrication process. Average total compensation for each worker amounted to about $16.00 per week, including the basic wage, family allowance, premiums earned under an incentive wage system, and payment for overtime. Beyond the normal eight-hour day, the employees worked two hours of overtime each day from Monday through Friday. They also worked 5 hours on Saturday--a total of 55 hours per week. Thus, average hourly earnings in the plant amount to about 30 cents per hour. When a management representative was asked whether or not a collective bargaining contract was in force, the answer (and not without pride) was in the negative, and the reason given was that the plant paid higher wages than those stipulated in contracts in this branch of industry.

The comparatively low wage structure clearly shows why the most important demand of workers at the bargaining table is for higher wages. Many Spanish employers, however, take a dim view of raising wages, believing that wage increases should be matched by a corresponding increase in productivity. The typical dialogue at the bargaining table involving wages and productivity points up an almost insoluble problem, based upon several crucial elements. First, since they are paid a low wage, Spanish workers cannot be expected to be eager workers. "Why give a fair day's work, " they ask, "when we do not get a fair day's wages?" As a Spanish writer puts it: ". . . since wages are low, the employees feel that they should

produce at a low level to correspond to low salaries."[42] In
fact, in some Spanish agreements, employers pay bonuses if
employees measure up to "normal" production levels, offer-
ing incentive wage systems over and above these bonuses.
Second, it is questionable that productivity can increase much
even if workers do extend themselves to the utmost; the capital equipment in most plants is not modern and efficient.   The
small size of practically all Spanish firms is an element of
the problem.   Since the typical plant employs less than 10
workers which reflects its limited financial resources, the
employer often cannot purchase new equipment to replace an-
tiquated methods; if he does, he faces the possibility that the
Ministry of Labor might not approve layoffs.   This inhibits
new investment that would increase productivity and allow for
wage increases.   Third, an important feature of the wage-
productivity problem is the fact that too many Spanish employers are not much concerned with increasing productivity even
if they can afford to do so.   In commenting on the generally
low productivity levels within Spanish industry, a Spanish
writer states:

> . . . the low yield of our production is attributable
> in general to Spanish business, content with its as-
> sured income, it is not concerned sufficiently to
> modernize its plants, and operating in a political
> structure which protects their interests, it has
> lost the opportunity to bring our nation to the lev-
> el of the rest of the European nations.[43]

Here then is the vicious circle which surrounds the wage-
productivity problem in collective bargaining.   This is aptly
put by a contemporary Spanish writer:

> . . . employers . . . oppose in principle, all in-
> creases in salaries if they are not accompanied by

---

[42]Javier M. de Bedoya, "Retribución y Productividad
en Los Convenios Colectivos," Revista de Política Social,
Instituto de Estudios Políticos, Madrid, V. 55, July, 1962,
p. 21.

[43]Julian Ariza Ricoi, "Convenios Colectivos,"Cuadernos
Para El Diálogo, Madrid, No. 10-11, July-August, 1964, p.
9.

an increase in productivity. The workers respond that the increase of productivity is not the mere condition of greater physical effort, and the employer should make the business more efficient, establishing a firm of optimum size, improvement in machinery, and increasing its capital. 44

The circle is not to be broken by demanding greater physical effort from Spanish workers as a prerequisite to higher wages. This route leads down a blind alley because of sharp limitations on how much higher productivity levels employees can achieve by their own efforts. To lift up oneself by pulling at one's bootstraps is an impossibility. That Spanish workers are as productive as any other workers, given a modern and efficient work plant, is testified to clearly by the fact that Spanish workers are in demand in other European nations and in South America, with about 350,000 Spaniards now working in European nations. If they were not productive, they would not be wanted. Instead of placing the responsibility for low productivity and low wages on the shoulders of Spanish workers, Spanish business and government must assume the challenge. They must take measures to promote productivity and to assure that the fruits of increasing productivity be shared fairly by the Spanish labor force.

44Héctor Maravall, op cit., p. 55.

CHAPTER **5** COLLECTIVE
BARGAINING:
SPANISH STYLE II

THE PRICE INCREASE DISCLAIMER

As a defense against wage-induced inflation, the Spanish collective bargaining law provides a procedure to discourage agreements that could lead to price increases. After a contract has been agreed to by the employer and employee representatives, they must decide whether or not the contract, as a whole, or any of its clauses, will result in a price increase. If their judgment is in the negative, the law requires their statement to that effect in the agreement. A typical contractual clause reads: "The parties who have arrived at this agreement judge that the application of the contract will not result in an increase of prices of the products of the Company."[1] With this disclaimer, the contract may be put into effect provided that the Ministry of Labor subsequently approves the agreement.

On the other hand, if either or both parties believe that the contract will increase prices, the contemplated price increase must be approved by the Spanish Commission on Economic Affairs. Without such approval the contract may not be put into effect. This commission, with Franco as Chairman, is composed of ministers of the various ministries of the Spanish government that deal with economic affairs primarily-- finance, commerce, labor and the like. The request for permission to raise prices is made in a petition submitted by the National Delegation of Syndicates, together with a report of the National Syndical Economic Council. If the Commission on Economic Affairs does not act on the petition within 20 days, it is assumed that it has tacitly approved the price increase. However, if the commission disapproves the price increase, this decision is forwarded to the National Delegation of Syndi-

---

[1]Guia y Compendio de Los Convenios Colectivos en España, Asociación Para El Progreso de La Dirección, Madrid, 1962, p. 272.

cates.   The parties to the contract are required to remove or change those clauses that are regarded as inflationary, and then to forward the agreement again to the Commission on Economic Affairs for its approval.

The Spanish government apparently has believed that this is an effective method to prevent collective bargaining from being an inflationary force in the economy.   Before other nations adopt this procedure, however, careful attention must be paid to the Spanish experience.   The fact is that the provision has proved to be worthless as an anti-inflationary measure.   Although the parties rarely indicate that their agreements will increase prices, there are many ways for employers to increase prices despite the disclaimer.   At times they increase prices while the negotiation is going on, as a hedge against any wage increase that subsequently may be agreed to by the parties.   Protracted negotiations particularly give an employer ample time to increase prices.   Once a company executes a disclaimer he may not subsequently raise prices and argue that the reason for this action is the collective bargaining contract.   However, this legal sanction is easily evaded, since employers can increase prices after the agreement goes into effect and claim that the price increase was attributable to other factors; for example, an increase in the cost of raw material.   Policing such conduct is virtually impossible because of the large number of contracts and firms.   In September, 1964, over 4, 000 collective agreements covered about 1, 620, 346 industrial, service, and agricultural establishments. [2] There simply are not enough inspectors or other law enforcement   officers to perform this police action. Further, the burden of proof would be on the government to show that the price increase did not result from other factors and was attributable to the collective bargaining agreement.   Clearly, the administrative impossibility of effective policing means that employers with virtual impunity may avoid the price disclaimer feature of the law.

An additional method of evasion reflects employer gamesmanship of the first order.   The Ministry of Labor breaks any impasse in negotiations through the process of compulsory arbitration.   Assume that the employer is determined to increase

---

[2]"Estadística General de Los   Convenios   Sindicales Desde La Promulgación de La Ley (1958) Hasta El 30 de Junio de 1964, " Vicesecretaria Nacional de Ordenación Social,   Organización Sindical Española, p. 1.

prices and, hence, does not desire to execute the disclaimer. All that he has to do is refuse to agree to a contract and thereby cause the intervention of the Ministry of Labor. Once the Ministry of Labor settles the contractual conflict by compulsory arbitration, the employer can then increase prices. Nothing prevents a price increase after a contract is put into effect through the system of governmental compulsory arbitration. Hence, the employer becomes the "reluctant dragon" and argues that the price increase was not of his making but that of the government.

INFLATION AND COLLECTIVE BARGAINING

Even though the Spanish employer may utilize these loopholes to increase prices, it does not necessarily follow that he has an economic justification for his action. Rather, the basis for price increases could be profiteering, instead of the economic content of the collective bargaining agreement. Indeed, in consideration of the sharp increase in Spain's consumer price index that began in 1963, the fundamental reasons for the current inflation, and wage and productivity data, one may safely conclude that collective bargaining does not account for the soaring price level.

From 1960 through 1963, industrial wages increased 53 per cent and productivity-output per man-hour increased 28.3 per cent. In the same time period, the consumer price index increased 15.9 per cent with real wages increasing by about 30 per cent. Before one concludes that these data contain evidence of wage-push inflation, one must assess the fundamental factors that have induced Spain's recent inflation. The current wave of inflation has focused attention on the nation's system of collective bargaining, and in some quarters, the verdict is that collective bargaining has been responsible. On this

---

3Indicadores Económicos, Instituto Nacional de Estadística, July-August, 1964. Data contained in the monthly bulletin published by the Spanish Syndical Organization (Estadísticas de Producción Industrial) compare closely to those reported by the Spanish National Institute of Statistics. For the time period under consideration, the Spanish Syndical Organization reports that wages increased 55.2 per cent; output per man hour, by 26.5 per cent; and real wages, by 31.5 per cent.

basis, some speculate that the collective bargaining system is threatened with extinction, and some advocate controls on the wage feature of the contracts. In November, 1964, the Spanish government announced a wage control plan, which will subsequently be assessed in this study.

Spain has indeed experienced a sharp increase in prices. Almost every day the daily press reflects on this problem, and there has been a flood of explanations and recommendations by government officials. The basis for the concern arises from the sharp upward swing of the consumer price index starting in January, 1963. From January, 1963, until September, 1964, Spain's consumer price index increased by 12. 7 per cent; from September, 1963, until September, 1964, it increased by 9. 1 per cent; and from January, 1964, until September, 1964, it increased by 7. 2 per cent. [4] Whatever wage-push inflation that might be in effect must be placed in juxtaposition to fundamental factors involved in the current wave of inflation. Such an analysis demonstrates that Spain's present inflationary problem is not rooted to wage increases or collective bargaining but rather is a product of a variety of elements.

Without attempting to establish the rank of relative importance, it can be demonstrated that these elements include: a high degree of monopoly in the area of distribution, wholesaling, and in some lines of industrial products; excessive investment in capital goods as a result of Spain's plan for economic development; a price support program for agricultural products; and tourism. On October 20, 1964, the then Minister of Commerce, Alberto Ullastres, identified three of these factors; he did not mention tourism but it is evident that the demand for food and services by 13, 000, 000 tourists per year in a nation with a total population of 31, 000, 000 must bring up prices. Of course, Spain must encourage tourism in order to acquire the foreign exchange it vitally needs to buttress its economy. This incongruity yields some conflict in the Spanish economy.

It is significant that the Minister of Commerce did not identify wages or collective bargaining as motivators of inflation. In fact, he stated that "not only have I not resisted wage increases, but I have taken the initiative in order to continue the rise in wages. "[5] Further, the Minister of Labor, Jesús

---

4Ibid., October 30, 1964.

5Ya (Madrid), October 20, 1964.

Romeo Gorria, on October 15, 1964, emphatically stated that to attribute the recent price increase exclusively to salaries is "to ignore the realities of the Spanish economy."[6] He further pointed out that the increase in Spanish productivity has not been exceeded by the wage increases and used as his point of reference data published by the National Institute of Statistics for 1962, 1963, and the first quarter of 1964. On the basis of this analysis, and affirming that continued wage increases represent a wholesome feature of Spain's program for economic development and the "fulfillment of the government policy to improve the conditions of labor in the country," he proclaimed flatly that "I am absolutely against any position which serves to block wage increases. The stagnation of wages signifies the freezing of social progress which must proceed of necessity parallel with economic progress." In the same month, José Soliz Ruiz, the highest official (National Delegate) of the Spanish Syndical Organization, the Secretary General of the Falange, and a member of Franco's cabinet, did not disagree with a resolution adopted by leaders of the national syndicates vigorously denouncing "the claim held in some quarters that the collective agreements are the sole cause of the recent increases in prices." This resolution affirmed that the agreements were practically "blameless" for the current inflation, pointing out that there were more fundamental causes for this situation.[7] Soliz presided over the meeting attended by the chiefs of the Spanish national syndicates when the resolution was adopted. At about the same time, Pedro Lamata Mejias, Secretary General of the Spanish Syndical Organization, and who, unlike Soliz, devotes full time to the Syndical Organization, stated in Barcelona that he disagreed "absolutely that the collective agreements are the cause for the increase of prices."[8]

In the light of these statements of very high ranking government officials, one might expect the Spanish government to attack the inflation problem on dimensions other than collective bargaining and wages. These ranking officials do not suggest wage controls as a corrective measure, and do state that collective bargaining and recent wage trends are at the most, incidental factors for the inflation.

---

[6]ABC (Madrid), October 15, 1964.

[7]Valladolid (Valladolid), October 2, 1964.

[8]Solidaridad Nacional (Barcelona), October 4, 1964.

WAGE-CONTROL POLICY

Yet, despite these declarations, on November 20, 1964, the government announced a policy of wage controls that will tend to worsen the position of Spanish labor. On this date the Spanish Commission on Economic Affairs announced the following policies relative to wage determination under collective bargaining, to be implemented by the Ministry of Labor: (1) wages will be increased when the consumer price index goes up by more than 3 per cent in a given time period; and (2) the maximum wage increase which workers can hope to get under collective bargaining is that which is matched by an increase in productivity.[9] In justifying this wage control program, a high ranking official of the Ministry of Labor, the Secretary General for Technical Affairs, made an almost incredible statement, declaring that wage increases that exceed productivity would most certainly increase prices in an economy (i.e., Spain), which "has a great deal of monopoly."[10] This most remarkable statement from the Ministry of Labor admits that monopolistic control of prices exists in Spain; recommends that nothing be done to promote competition; and advises that wage policy must adjust to the fact of monopoly. Note the reference to monopoly as an inflationary force in Spain by the Minister of Commerce made only about one month before the policy of wage controls was announced. Though the representative of the Ministry of Labor does not necessarily speak for the Spanish government, his ready acceptance of monopoly probably reflects the outlook of some of its highest officers, and his statement tends to show that the Spanish government apparently would rather adjust its wage policy to the situation than embark upon an effective policy of freeing its economy from monopolistic elements.

This wage policy and the government's apparent acceptance of monopolistic interests should be assessed in the light of the distribution of Spain's national income. In 1963, 60.7 per cent of the labor force received only 39.1 per cent of the

---

[9]Ya (Madrid), November 20, 1964.

[10]Pueblo (Madrid), November 21, 1964.

national income, and 39.3 per cent of the labor force received 60.9 per cent of the national income. [11] The 39.3 per cent figure includes about 2 million self-employed farmers and thousands of small shopkeepers, whose incomes are very low. When these adjustments are made, a Lorenz curve would demonstrate that only a fraction of the Spanish people receive the lion's share of the national income. Indeed, wage compensation as a share of the national income has actually declined between 1955 and 1962. The wage share was calculated as 52 per cent in 1955 and 51.7 per cent in 1962. [12] Thus, despite the fact that real wages for Spanish workers have increased about 30 per cent for the period 1960-1963, the over-all economic program of the Spanish government, of which the current wage control policy is now an important element, in the words of a Spanish writer, "tends to sharpen the difference between classes, making the rich much more rich, and the poor a little less poor."[13]

Unfortunately, Spanish workers do not have the capacity to take any effective action to protest against a government policy which is against their best interests. To whom do they turn for relief from a wage policy which is bound to impair their economic position? The most they can hope for is a real wage increase based upon productivity increases. This

---

[11]The distribution of Spain's national income is somewhat a mystery, because different agencies of the Spanish government report different statistics. The data used above are those reported by the Spanish government Development Plan Commission. See Summary of the Spanish Economic and Social Development Plan, 1964-1967, Commission of the Government Development Plan, Office of Public Relations, Madrid, 1964, pp. 14-15.

[12]Contabilidad Nacional de España, Ministerio de Hacienda, 1964, p. 16. It reports the following, showing labor's share of the national income: 1955, 52 per cent; 1958, 48.6 per cent; 1959, 49.8 per cent; 1960, 49.5 per cent; 1961, 49.0 per cent; and 1962, 51.7 per cent. (The last two years are not reported in the volume cited; however, data for 1961 and 1962 are found in other reports of the Ministerio de Hacienda.)

[13]Julian Ariza Ricoi, "Convenios Colectivos," Cuadernos Para El Diálogo, Madrid, No. 10-11, July-August, 1964, p. 9.

kind of a "guideline" approach is even attacked in the United States by the American labor movement as well as by many responsible American economists as inequitable and unworkable. However, in the light of the extremely low wages of the Spanish workers, the unwillingness of many Spanish employ - ers to improve their plants, and the sharp inequity of national income, the policy does not reflect social and economic justice.

Who is to be the spokesman for the Spanish worker? Here is the Minister of Labor stating in October, 1964, that he is "absolutely against any position which serves to block wage increases," and who with apparent equanimity completely reversed his ground one month later to implement the contemporary wage control program. Indeed, the Ministry of Labor circulated a letter in the summer of 1964, to all personnel empowered to review negotiated agreements, directing them to disapprove any contract which provided for a wage increase beyond 5 per cent. Note that this circular was dispatched before the Spanish government announced its November, 1964, wage control policy, and before the Minister of Labor made his celebrated October, 1964, statement affirming his position not to block wage increases. It was understandably impossible to obtain a copy of the letter. That it was issued and implemented, however, is corroborated by unimpeachable sources. After the Minister of Labor publicly declared that he was opposed to a wage restraint program, a large number of workers' representatives, many from the provinces, called upon him in Madrid to lend their moral support to his program and to thank him for his statement, little suspecting that the Minister of Labor a few months before had circulated the wage-hold directive.

And what of the Spanish Syndical Organization, which despite its schizophrenic character, is supposed to spend at least 50 per cent of its energy on workers' interests? Reference was made to the judgment of its two highest officers who, in effect, held wage increases blameless for the current wave of inflation only one month before the current wage policy was put into effect. No evidence exists that the Spanish Syndical Organization intends to protest or take any action whatsoever against the current policy. In effect, they cannot, because they are appointed to their jobs by the Spanish government. Indeed, if any further evidence is needed that the Spanish Syndical Organization does not represent the best interests of the Spanish workers, and that it is an instrument of the Spanish government, such proof is clearly demonstrated by its acquiesence to a wage policy which is patently inequitable. The cold and irrefutable fact is that the Spanish workers do not have an effective forum through which to protest. Frozen to a "trade union" movement which is an instrument of the government, they are helpless to raise their voices against policies which are contrary to their best interests.

POWERS OF THE MINISTRY OF LABOR

Clearly, these observations on the November, 1964, wage control policy, as well as other features of Spanish law already discussed, demonstrate that the Spanish system simply does not permit effective self-determination of working conditions, but is a system of collective bargaining under the auspices of the Spanish government. True, Spanish employer and employee representatives are free to negotiate the terms of agreements; however, depending upon the shifts of governmental policy, the agreements must conform to predetermined governmental objectives. Perhaps when inflationary pressures in Spain subside, the current wage control policy will be abolished. Regardless, the 1964 wage restriction program demonstrates all too clearly that the government can impose contractual controls at its pleasure.

Under the terms of Spanish law, the Ministry of Labor must approve every agreement before it can go into effect. When the agreement is provincial in scope, approval must be sought from the Delegado Provincial (Provincial Delegate), the top ranking representative of the Ministry of Labor in each of the 50 provinces. If the contract is interprovincial, approval must be obtained from the Office of the Director General of Labor, which is part of the Ministry of Labor located, of course, in Madrid. Since November, 1964, all agreements are forwarded to Madrid to determine whether the agreement meets the standards of the Ministry of Labor. That this procedure violates the collective bargaining law, which specifically provides that provincial agreements are to be approved by the Provincial Delegates, shows that expediency rather than the rule of law is a characteristic of administration of this statute.

The power to approve agreements also means the power to reject negotiated agreements, and the law specified conditions under which the Ministry of Labor or its representatives may disapprove agreements. This disapproval may be incurred when it is determined that either of the parties has engaged in coercion, fraudulent, or bad faith conduct. Under these circumstances, the entire contract is disapproved, and if the party judged guilty of such conduct is the requestor of negotiations, it may not be permitted to seek permission to negotiate an a-greement for six months. If the other party engages in such conduct, the Ministry of Labor is authorized to write the terms of the agreement.

Disapproval may occur when the Ministry of Labor determines that certain procedural standards were not followed relative to the initiation of negotiations or in the contract deliberations. For example, the Ministry of Labor will not approve a contract if the party which sought negotiations did not obtain approval to begin negotiations from the Spanish Syndical Organization.

A third reason for disapproval is the presence of provisions that diminish the rights of workers as established in the minimum labor standards. If a reglamentación provides for more favorable terms for employees than the agreement, it must prevail over the terms of the contract. Thus, "collective bargaining agreements may improve on standards established by law, or may apply where the legal decrees do not cover some working condition."[14] Apparently, the Ministry of Labor has a tough administrative problem in deciding whether a reglamentación or an agreement provides "more favorable conditions." For example, what should be the decision if a labor agreement provides more beneficial conditions for a comparatively large group of employees, but wherein the arrangements impair the rights of a few workers as established under a particular reglamentación? As expressed by an outstanding Spanish labor expert, "it is a difficult problem at times to determine in practice which is the situation most favorable to the workers. . . ."[15]

In any event, collective bargaining agreements are to be superimposed over the system of minimum labor standards, the foundation upon which the agreements are to establish better working conditions. On this basis, it could be argued that this system tends to make collective bargaining agreements comparatively less important in the Spanish labor relations system. The collective bargaining agreement is not the alternative to the play of the labor market. The reglamentaciones

---

[14]José Pérez Leñero, Convenios Colectivos Sindicales: Doctrina y Legislación, Madrid, 1959, p. 21.

[15]Ibid., p. 89.

stand between the labor market and collective agreements as a defensive posture to workers' interests. It would appear on the surface at least that the syndicates that do not posses executive power in the establishment of the Ministry of Labor minimum labor standards would be in favor of their elimination. Whereas the collective bargaining agreements are negotiated within the framework of the Spanish Syndical Organization, it has only a consultive function in the formation of the reglamentaciones. With the elimination of the system of minimum labor standards, the only alternative to wage and working condition determination by market forces would be the collective bargaining agreement. Under these circumstances, the prestige of the Spanish Syndical Organization and the collective bargaining agreement would tend to increase . The syndicate system and collective bargaining would tend to be more attractive to and more crucial to the Spanish workers. In the absence of collective agreements, their working conditions would be determined unilaterally by the employer with his decisions in this respect being conditioned only by the labor market and his conceptions of social justice and humanitarianism.

Despite the merits of this analysis as a possible means of increasing the prestige of collective bargaining and the syndical organization, the officials of the Spanish Syndical Organization are not in favor of abolishing the system of minimum labor standards. They urge the retention of the reglamentaciones or some other system of legally imposed minimum labor standards. Recently the syndical organization has speculated that some new instrument of the state should establish minimum labor standards. In the light of the struggle between the Spanish Syndical Organization and the Ministry of Labor for the primary position in the establishment of Spanish working conditions, it is likely that the syndicates would welcome the erosion of power of the Ministry of Labor. In any event, the Spanish Syndical Organization appointed officials desire that a legal foundation be retained on which the collective bargaining agreement may serve to improve working conditions.

The reason for their attitude is easy to explain. If collective bargaining were to represent the only defensive mechanism of worker interests, this situation could lead to the destruction of the Spanish Syndical Organization in its present form. With the elimination of state established minimums, the workers' sections of the syndicates would be required to assume a truly militant role reflecting independent unionism. This, of course, would strike a telling blow against the current syndical structure which is supposed simultaneously to reconcile the interests of the workers and the employers. Militant trade unionism of an independent character is simply not compatible with the theory and practice of the Spanish Syndical Organization. Aware of these circumstances, and aware further that the Spanish government is opposed to independent unionism in any form whatsoever, the appointed Spanish syndical leaders understandably must oppose any development in which the syndical system would shed its schizophrenic character. They must preserve the current system or face dismissal. Militant worker groups must be prevented at any cost.

The Ministry of Labor will disapprove an agreement for a fourth reason; that is, if it includes companies not embraced by a reglamentación. This proscription refers to the kinds of bargaining units permitted under the collective bargaining statute. As stated, an agreement may cover a single firm, different firms in the same province, or different employers who operate in two or more provinces. However, at all times, the company or companies embraced by a collective bargaining agreement must be included within the scope of one or more particular minimum labor standards.

Furthermore, contracts will be disapproved if they include provisions that modify or conflict with any of the powers of the state, interfere with "social peace and discipline", or contain clauses that tend to interfere with the "cooperative" character of human relations within the firm. This vague wording permits arbitrary interpretation by the Ministry of Labor to allow for disapproval of almost any collective agreement. The wording of the statute confers upon the Ministry of Labor exclusive power to interpret its terms, including, of course, the practical application of such ambiguous language.

When fraud, coercion, or bad faith are involved in negotiation, the parties will not have the opportunity to rectify their conduct. However, where the agreement is disapproved for any of the other reasons, the Ministry of Labor will return the agreement to the parties, who will have the opportunity to take action to remove or correct objectionable clauses.

COMPULSORY ARBITRATION

The Ministry of Labor is also empowered to break any impasse between the parties; to break any deadlock in negotiations, a system of compulsory arbitration is established. The arbitrator is the government: the parties may not use the services of a private arbitrator, and no provision in the law permits either party to appeal to the courts in case it believes the award to be against its best interests. The award of the Ministry of Labor is final and binding.

Such a system of compulsory arbitration is the antithesis of free collective bargaining. It is not voluntary arbitration, wherein the parties elect to submit their disputes to arbitration; they are forced to submit their unresolved differences to the government for final determination. The Ministry of Labor is not compelled to arbitrate disputes. Perhaps the authors of the statute believed that by providing some discretion to the Ministry of Labor in this respect, the parties would be more prone to arrive at an agreement without arbitration. Though experience has demonstrated that the Ministry of Labor only infrequently has refused to break deadlocks by arbitration, this feature of the law has been criticized in some quarters. In advocating that the Ministry of Labor should be compelled to arbitrate any dispute submitted to it, a Spanish writer states: ". . . it is just to state that experience justifies some reforms to the law, and among them, the most important, the necessity of imposing arbitration, since without it the danger exists that the law could become ineffective, since any of the parties to a negotiation would be able to refuse to negotiate if they know definitely that the Ministry of Labor does not have the obligation to resolve the dispute by arbitration and there only exists the possibility that the Ministry may dictate a decision."[16] Even the Secretary General of the Spanish Syndical Organization criticized the law in this respect and further underscored the desire of the syndicates for more and not less governmental control of labor relations.[17] Along the same lines, the National Syndicate for Cattle referred to this feature of the law when it recommended that when the employer does not appear at a collective bargaining negotiation, the Ministry of Labor "shall be obligated

---

[16]José Manuel Mateu de Ros, "El Convenio Colectivo, Instrumento de Unidad y Conviencia," Jornal, Organo de Difusión Sindicalista, Organización Sindical Española, Servición de Relaciones Exteriores, Madrid, No. 80, April-May, 1960, p. 223.

[17]Pedro Lamata Mejias, "El Sindicato y La Contratación Laboral," Jornal, V. 80, April-May, 1960, p. 226.

to dictate a decision within two months. . ."[18]

Such criticism is quite understandable and indeed justified under the framework of Spanish labor relations law.   If the Ministry of Labor refuses to arbitrate a dispute, the work - ers, forbidden to strike, have no opportunity to force an a- greement. Under these circumstances, there will be no con- tract, and the employer's position in effect is upheld.

That the Spanish system of collective bargaining pro- vides for compulsory arbitration and to this extent is not compatible with a system of free collective bargaining has not been unnoticed by Spanish labor experts. Thus, "the law acknowledges the intervention of the State in cases of disa- greement. If state intervention in this respect is excessive, the collective agreement system will reflect the system of reglamentaciones, the only exception being that state decrees to break deadlocks will refer only to the parties directly in- volved in the negotiation, while the reglamentación has a wid- er effect."[19] It may be added that even if the government is prudent in its role of breaking deadlocks in negotiations, it establishes state precedents which undoubtedly serve as pat- terns for other negotiations. In this manner, the principle of flexibility, and the avowed desire to free labor relations from state determination--a basic objective of the law--tends to be unrealized.   In short, as long as a system of compulsory ar- bitration exists wherein the state serves as the arbitrator, the route to the achievement of an agreement simply does   not represent the play of the free will of the parties.

Indeed, recent trends indicate that a growing number of agreements are being put in force by decrees of the Ministry of Labor. For the years 1959 through 1962, the Spanish Syn- dical Organization reports a   total of 115 instances in which the parties were unable to reach an agreement at the bargain- ing table. However, from 1963 and the final 9 months of 1964, the number of these instances totaled 222. The chief reason for this is that wages are comparatively higher than in former years. Accordingly, employers are assuming a stiffer atti- tude at the bargaining table with the result of forcing more disputes into compulsory arbitration. On the basis of this trend, it appears likely that the Ministry of Labor's power of compulsory arbitration will be used much more frequently in

---

[18]Ya (Madrid), March 26, 1964.

[19]José Pérez Leñero, op. cit. , p. 24.

future years. To this extent, the Spanish collective bargaining system will reflect less and less of free will and a proportionately greater degree of state intervention.

STATUS AND PRESTIGE OF SPANISH AGREEMENTS

It has been noted that the system of state imposed minimum labor standards tends to detract from the prestige of Spanish collective bargaining agreements, because these state regulations provide an alternative method for workers to achieve a measure of protection from the play of the labor market and from employer unilateral determination of working conditions. In still another way the system of reglamentaciones tends to detract from the prestige and status of the collective bargaining system. During the effective term of a collective bargaining contract, the Ministry of Labor may announce a change in a minimum labor standard that would apply to companies that have already negotiated a collective bargaining contract as well as to those that operate without agreements.

Once a revision in an existing reglamentación is put into effect, it applies equally to both categories of firms. Then, what occurs when a new minimum labor standard provides for better working conditions than those contained in collective bargaining contracts? The Ministry of Labor provided the answer to this problem on July 5, 1962, by directing that in this situation the contract may be reopened and the improved conditions put into effect. Such an arrangement, of course, tends not only to detract from the prestige of collective agreements, but establishes a disruptive force in collective bargaining. An employer may have made concessions on the expectation that the state will not change the standards included in the collective bargaining contract. Furthermore, the workers have an opportunity to display gamesmanship. Their representatives may agree to the terms of a labor agreement, and immediately thereafter push for a change in the reglamentación applying to their branch of industry to improve on the conditions established in the agreement. Here, of course, is evidence of bad faith on the workers' part, but such gamesmanship is perfectly legal under the existing Spanish law. Another feature is involved in such tactics. Workers may wait until the state announces a new and improved minimum labor standard before taking the initiative to negotiate a labor agree-

ment.   This conduct is facilitated if their channel of communication to the Ministry of Labor via the syndical system alerts
them to an impending change.

More serious, however, than these considerations is
that workers may demand to have the entire contract reopened
for new negotiations after a new minimum labor standard has
been put into effect, despite the fact that the July, 1962, order
precisely states that the new standards will supercede only
those provisions of the agreement that are embraced by its
terms; the other provisions are not to be changed during the
effective period.   For example, the Ministry of Labor may
announce a better vacation program than is included in a collective bargaining contract.   Under this circumstance, the
collective bargaining contract may be changed only to include
the vacation program.

In practice, however, workers frequently use this circumstance as a wedge to change the entire labor agreement.
What might appear incongruous, moreover, is that employers
frequently agree to negotiate an entirely new agreement to
allay employee dissension and possible slowdowns--more difficult for employers to control than an outright strike.   Thus,
if employees implement a sophisticated slowdown activity,
they can use this illegal tactic as an effective weapon to harass
the employer into agreeing to negotiate a new labor contract.

Closely allied to such employee conduct, but of greater
importance in demonstrating employee irresponsibility, is the
fact that employees frequently arbitrarily denounce an existing agreement during its effective term and demand the negotiation of a new agreement.   This type of denunciation is independent from any change in a minimum labor standard which
provides at least a crack in the door as the basis for the negotiation of a new agreement before the expiration date.   Under the terms of the Spanish law, all agreements run for two
years unless the parties agree to some other length of the contract's effective operation.   In practice, most contracts are
negotiated for a two-year period.   If either party desires to
change an agreement, the law stipulates that at least a three-
month notice must be provided.   In the absence of a timely
notice, the law provides that the agreement is tacitly extended.

Experience has demonstrated, however, that in violation of the law and of the terms of their own agreements, employees frequently and arbitrarily denounce contracts and demand new negotiations.   Even the Spanish system of authoritarian labor relations does not prevent employees from suc-

cessfully using this strategy. That this kind of conduct is actually a serious problem, and is not just academic, is made quite clear by pertinent observations by labor experts. One writer comments: "if the workers' representatives are truly authentic, when an agreement is signed it obligates the workers with the same force which binds the employer". [20] A Madrid daily newspaper editorially observes that if agreements can be radically changed or broken during their period of effectiveness and before their termination date, this results in a "blow to the entire system of collective agreements, and the stability necessary for the system of collective agreements would disappear to the prejudice of all." [21]

Several factors may motivate such action on the part of the workers. Undoubtedly, the chief reason is their irresponsibility and their lack of understanding of the character of the collective bargaining process. However, although their conduct cannot be condoned, other considerations tend to explain their action. Employees do not have the opportunity to elect special representatives to negotiate their agreements, and sometimes resent the official representatives, manifesting their discontent in premature denunciation of the agreement. This would be particularly true if the syndical elections do not reflect the free choice of the workers. Workers, moreover, do not have the opportunity to vote on the acceptance of a contract, but must take the contract accepted by their syndical representatives. Probably, if workers had the chance to ratify the agreement, they would be more likely to adhere to its terms. In addition, the recent sharp increase in the consumer price index might prompt workers to break agreements: with wages frozen for the contract period, the sharp increase in prices erodes their purchasing power, and this factor is conducive to labor conflict. Finally, their action might be sparked by general discontent with the state controlled and operated syndical system. Workers, forced to become members of and pay dues to the syndical organization have no legal means to express their resentment of the situation. Their breaking of agreements might be interpreted as an indirect method of demonstrating their general antipathy to the Spanish Syndical

---

[20]Emilio Torres Gallego, "El Diálogo en El Mundo de Trabajo," Cuadernos Para El Diálogo, Madrid, No. 10-11, July-August, 1964.

[21]Ya (Madrid), September 4, 1964.

Organization.

Another feature of the Spanish law raises a serious doubt as to whether the Spanish government really intends that collective bargaining be elevated to a position of predominance within the nation. Employers and employees are free to make individual agreements; notwithstanding the established conditions of employment, the employer may award better terms to individual workers. Accordingly, the contract does not establish the common rule in the plant, an indispensable feature of traditional trade unionism, but the agreement may only serve to be the stepping stone which may be improved upon by unilateral employer conduct. Individual agreements which contain better conditions of employment take precedence over the collective bargaining contract. Not only does such an arrangement tend to undermine the prestige of collective bargaining, but could serve as the basis of employer discrimination among workers and for invidious employee comparisons which would be inimical to a sound labor relations program at the plant level.

To underscore the provision of the law which subordinates collective agreements to those of an individual character, the Ministry of Labor on July 28, 1958, stated that "collective agreements must be considered as occupying an intermediate place between the reglamentaciones and the individual contract." In short, collective bargaining is not to be regarded as the chief instrument of labor relations policy. Rather, the terms of the agreement provide only a sort of away station for more favorable individual agreements. Clearly, such a system does not endow collective bargaining with prestige and seriously reduces its potential as an effective instrument of labor relations policy.

CHAPTER **6** EVALUATION OF THE
SPANISH COLLECTIVE
BARGAINING SYSTEM

WIDESPREAD USAGE

If the standard upon which the Spanish collective bargaining system is to be judged is widespread usage, the evidence reveals that it has been successful. Usage of the law
developed very slowly. Before 1961, there were only 346 contracts in existence and which covered only 569,135 workers. [1]
Other than the newness of the system and the natural breaking-
in period, two major factors account for this early slow development. In the first place, as expected, employers did not
receive the law with enthusiasm. They were accustomed to
the system of reglamentaciones, and, as stated, the standards
established by these legal decrees are quite low. It is always
difficult to break with the past, particularly when traditional
methods serve a vested interest. One explanation of the slow
development of use of the law reports that upon its passage
the statute "was accepted fully by the workers. However, employers received it with a certain scepticism and in some
places with marked hostility. "[2]
Much more important, however, was the economic climate of Spain during the first few years of the law's operation.
Some background will help the reader to understand the situation that prevailed prior to 1961. In May, 1956, the Spanish
government by legal decree raised wages for industrial workers by an amount ranging from 20 to 30 per cent. This across-
the-board wage increase sparked an unprecedented inflation.
By August of that year prices had increased by 30 per cent or
more. This is not the place to examine the fundamental rea-

---

[1]Revista de Legislación Social, No. 22, April, 1962, p.
105.

[2]Tiempo Nuevo, Madrid, V. 10, No. 121, May, 1964,
p. 72.

sons for the 1956 inflation. Informed judgment, however, attributes the price increase more to psychological factors and business profiteering than to basic economic circumstances. At this time, of course, wages in Spain were at very low levels--considerably lower than they are at the present time. Recall that it was not until 1963 that the $1.00 per day minimum wage law was put into effect. In short, the consensus among informed Spanish people, particularly economists, was that the business community took advantage of the wage increase and arbitrarily raised prices beyond that which was necessary in order to pass off to the consumer the entire increase in labor costs. It is said that many firms raised prices by 30 per cent or more, as if wage costs represented 100 per cent of total costs. [3]

The Spanish government quickly moved to combat the 1956 inflation. Price ceilings were put into effect, and firms were required to post prices for commodities and services. A corps of inspectors was authorized to enforce the price control program. (This recalls the price control program in the United States during World War II.) By July, 1959, the inflationary pressures had subsided, and in that month price ceilings were abandoned. However, at the same time, the Spanish government installed a tough stabilization program. The peseta was devalued from about 40 pesetas to the dollar to 60 pesetas to the dollar. Other important features of the stabilization program involved sharp restrictions on business credit and a balanced national budget.

Such a business and economic climate, of course, made it very difficult for employers to provide economic benefits in collective bargaining. Wage increases were hard to come by, and since an increased wage was then as now the primary demand of employees, Spanish workers did not register much enthusiasm for collective bargaining contracts. Why negoti-

---

[3] It is noteworthy that such economic piracy and illiteracy is still a problem under collective bargaining agreements. Thus, in 1964, a Madrid daily newspaper states that ". . . it is argued by employer interests that a raise of wages must result in the same rate of increase in prices. This viewpoint is unfortunately widely held. To double the rate of wages is not to double all the factors of the cost of production, and, therefore, it is not necessary to translate a given wage increase by the same percentage in prices." Ya (Madrid), September 4, 1964.

ate them if they could not improve the wage structure?

That the stabilization program was chiefly responsible for the slow development of collective bargaining agreements is affirmed by practically all observers of the Spanish scene. For example, in a studious and comprehensive article dealing with the development and current position of Spanish collective bargaining, the author states: ". . . the stabilization program did not present an economic climate favorable to the development and application of the [collective bargaining] system. Controls dedicated to the holding of the price line made the employers resist a great deal of the demands of workers. Hence, for the first two years of the law it was difficult to exploit its use."[4]

With the start of 1961, the stabilization program was relaxed, and that year a sharp increase in the number of collective bargaining agreements negotiated by Spanish employers and employees was noted. For 1961, 412 contracts were put into effect; for 1962, 1,713; and in 1963, 1,149 contracts were negotiated.[5] At the time of this writing, the most recent data available are those reported by the Spanish Syndical Organization as of September 30, 1964. At that time, a total of 4,532 collective bargaining agreements covered 5,338,777 workers and applied to 1,620,346 firms.[6] Of this amount, 2,009 agreements were negotiated in agriculture; 2,000 in industry; and 523 in service establishments. As of 1964, the total Spanish labor force amounted to about 13 million. About 3 million are not considered as proper subject for collective bargaining agreements in the same way that about 20 million of the United States labor force is not considered organizable. Thus, as of the fall of 1964, over 60 per cent of all Spanish "organizable" workers were covered by collective bargaining agreements. In comparison, United States experience demonstrates that about 30 per cent of organizable workers are in the American

---

[4]Héctor Maravall, "Las Negociaciones Colectivos," Revista de Política Social, Instituto Estudios Políticos, Madrid, V. 57, 1963, p. 45.

[5]Tiempo Nuevo, op. cit., p. 72.

[6]"Estadística General de Los Convenios Sindicales Desde La Promulgación de La Ley (1958) Hasta El 30 de Junio de 1964," Vicesecretaria Nacional de Ordenación Social, Organización Sindical Española, p. 1.

labor movement.

Whether or not the impressive trend of Spanish labor agreements exhibited in recent years will continue depends largely upon the government's wage policy. If workers believe that wage increase possibilities are to be blocked by the current wage control program, their enthusiasm to negotiate new agreements and/or to renew expiring labor agreements is likely to lessen. This was the state of affairs during Spain's stabilization program of 1959 to 1961, when the evidence clearly shows that workers did not exhibit much enthusiasm for collective bargaining agreements because the stabilization program made it very difficult to obtain wage increases. It is emphasized that higher wages is by far the chief benefit that Spanish workers hope to achieve in collective bargaining.

Indeed, there is some reason to believe that a slowdown in the number of negotiated agreements is already in evidence. It was in the third quarter of 1964--July through September-- that the current inflation in Spain clearly was manifest, and though the wage control program was not put into force until November, the Ministry of Labor during this period started to review all agreements as to their possible repercussions on prices, despite the fact that the parties included the necessary price disclaimer clause in their agreements. If the judgment were in the positive, the agreements were disapproved and dispatched back to the parties for renegotiation. Thus, for the third quarter of 1964, the Spanish Syndical Organization reports the negotiation and approval of 271 agreements as against 352 in the second quarter, and 289 for the first quarter, January through March. While this data is not conclusive evidence of waning confidence in the effectiveness of the collective bargaining system, it appears to be at least indicative of this attitude.

QUALITY OF THE AGREEMENTS

Another important standard of evaluation is the substantive quality of the agreements. Specifically, are Spanish workers in fact obtaining improved conditions of employment through the collective bargaining system? The recent upsurge of the number of agreements would indicate an affirmative answer. The meaningful standard of comparison would be the substance of the agreements as against the terms established in the system of reglamentaciones put into effect by the Ministry of Labor. It is beyond the scope of this study to make an accurate judgment in this respect. To do so would require a comparative analysis of the terms of the contracts with the reglamentaciones, a task which would easily require the writing of another study. Indeed, one wonders why such studies have not been made by proper agencies of the Spanish government, the Spanish Syndical Organization, or private investigators. At this writing, the only two studies along these lines show wage trends negotiated for 1963 within the agricultural, industrial, and service sectors of the Spanish economy. On the basis of these studies, it seems clear that negotiated wages are higher than those established by the reglamentaciones. [7]

Despite the results of these studies, and other general statements made to show the gains made by workers under collective bargaining contracts, [8] some Spanish observers judge that the improvement of working conditions of Spanish workers is not to be attributable to the system of collective bargaining. For example: ". . .we do not say that the agreements as a method to resolve the labor problem is worthless, but the experience of the last several years shows that the situation has not improved very much since 1958."[9] Such a point of view holds that the comparative prosperity of the last

---

[7]"La Tendencia Salarial en Los Convenios Colectivos," Organización Sindical Española, Vicesecretaria Nacional de Ordenación Social, June, 1964, p. 12.

[8]For example, a Spanish Syndical Organization statement claims general improvement of working conditions through collective bargaining: ". . . outstanding in the first place, are the successes obtained by the workers in the area of wages; also for special payments, July 18 and Christmas and vacations; these are higher in some agreements as compared with the legal minimums. Moreover, contracts exhibit some profit sharing and improvements in the area of social security." (Tiempo Nuevo, op. cit., p. 71.) However, the defect of statements such as these are their general and sweeping generalizations which do not contain a factual basis. As such, they do not contain the necessary proof upon which to base an irrefutable conclusion.

[9]Julian Ariza Ricoi, "Convenios Colectivos," Cuadernos Para El Diálogo, Madrid, No. 10-11, July-August, 1964, p. 9.

several years sparked by important additions to Spain's industrial plant (financed in part by the large-scale investment of American business), tourism, and the results of Spanish worker emigration to foreign nations are the fundamental factors for whatever improvement in working conditions Spanish workers are experiencing. Indeed, it is extremely doubtful that collective bargaining agreements could provide any meaningful improvement of Spanish working conditions if 350,000 Spanish workers were not employed in foreign nations, if 13 million tourists bypassed Spain, and if foreign investment in Spain's industrial plant ceased. These are vital props to the Spanish economy, and their curtailment would deal an almost fatal blow to the entire Spanish economy and would tend to make collective bargaining an academic exercise.

SPANISH WORKER EMIGRATION

Spain's collective bargaining system has not dampened the enthusiasm of Spanish workers to find jobs in foreign nations. Attracted by much higher wages, a steady stream of Spanish workers flows to foreign nations. Collective bargaining has not reduced the international wage differential which stimulates emigration. In the absence of the differential, it is doubtful that many Spanish workers would emigrate, because they find that cultural, religious, and language differences make working in foreign nations an unpleasant experience. These factors, beyond the disruption of family life, would prompt the Spanish worker to remain at home. Indeed, the Spanish government views emigration with mixed emotions. As a matter of national pride, it cannot fully approve emigration. On the other hand, the foreign exchange acquired by the process is recognized as a vital stabilizing influence of the Spanish economy; it is also true that emigration tends to lessen Spanish unemployment. Indeed, one barometer of the state of the Spanish economy and the effectiveness of collective bargaining is the rate of emigration in future years.

PRODUCTIVITY AND ILLEGAL STRIKES

Other barometers are available to evaluate the Spanish collective bargaining system. As stated, one objective of the

1958 labor law was to increase productivity. Collective bargaining was to introduce a measure of flexibility into the determination of working conditions which is not possible under
the system of reglamentaciones. As pointed out, output per
man hour increased in Spain by about 28 per cent for the years
1960 through 1963, or about 7 per cent per year. It is always
difficult to separate the elements that are involved in the productivity experience of a nation. In the case of Spain, recent
additions to its capital equipment probably is the chief factor.
Other features of recent Spanish development, including better education and health, likewise serve to bolster Spain's
productivity. Despite the impossibility of pinpointing the effect of collective bargaining on productivity, it is safe to conclude that it has been a positive factor. Though the collective
bargaining system is controlled by the government, employers
and employees have an opportunity to adjust working conditions
to the particular circumstances of the plant in contrast to the
inflexible and across-the-board impact of the system of reglamentaciones. As the World Bank reports: ". . .a recent development in the direction of greater flexibility is the widespread use of collective bargaining agreements. These make
it increasingly possible to relate wages to productivity at the
plant level. . ."[10] In short, the collective bargaining system
has served to increase Spanish productivity, though, of course,
it is impossible to assess the actual amount. However, it
must be noted that the future capacity for collective bargaining to continue to be a positive force in this respect will be
seriously impaired to the extent that the Spanish government
takes a firmer hold on the process. Policies such as the 1964
wage control program are not conducive to the maximizing of
the potential of collective bargaining as a positive productivity
force.

One should speculate on what the impact on productivity
would be if Spain legalized independent labor unions. Such a
movement would be bound to be more militant than the state-
controlled Spanish Syndical Organization whose policymakers
and chief officials are appointed by the government and who,
therefore, must submit to predetermined governmental policies. Many responsible American economists hold that one
factor for the ever increasing United States productivity is the

---

[10]The Economic Development of Spain, International
Bank for Reconstruction and Development (Baltimore: Johns
Hopkins Press, 1963), p. 345.

constant pressure of the American labor movement. Ever aware of this pressure, United States employers are stimulated to take appropriate measures to improve their plants. Undoubtedly, the same would be true in Spain under a system of free trade unionism.

Strikes, though illegal, occur in Spain. Several of the important strikes took place after the passage of the collective bargaining law. As a matter of fact, some Spanish experts maintain that a preponderance of strikes have occurred most frequently in those industries and areas in which collective agreements are comparatively the heaviest. Under the stimulus of these agreements and worker self-confidence gained by their negotiations, employees are more inclined to strike. To the extent that strikes occur, it is manifest that Spanish workers do not find the collective bargaining system an effective forum for the adjustment of working conditions. Strikes show that the contemporary collective bargaining system does not meet the needs of the Spanish worker.

The Spanish government tends to dismiss the strikes as temporary aberrations of the Spanish workers and as a reflection of the devices of "foreign agitators". This is a first-rate delusion, since strikes in Spain before and after the passage of the 1958 law reflect the frustration and the dissatisfaction by workers with their economic lot. If Spain's strikes are, in fact, the work of "foreign agitators", they have a bountiful vineyard in which to operate. If Spanish workers were content with their economic position, if they sincerely believed that the Spanish Syndical Organization and the collective bargaining system fundamentally served their interests, the clarion call of "foreign agitators" would fall on deaf ears. Let it be emphasized that it takes rare courage to strike in Spain. Unlike American workers who risk only their jobs and their unions, the Spanish worker risks imprisonment when he engages in a strike. When Spanish workers strike, it is clear that their frustrations are such that they are willing to risk their all in the effort to remedy social injustice.

It is very unlikely that the Franco government will ever fully legalize the strike. Though strike activity in Spain is based fundamentally upon economic conditions, the Franco regime believes that strike activity is a threat to the contemporary political structure of the government. Spain presents the incongruous situation wherein in a free enterprise and capitalistic system workers are denied the only effective weapon which they possess to play a meaningful part in the determination of working conditions. It is emphasized that Spain's economy is based fundamentally on capitalism and free enterprise. Thus, the "Spanish State has pursued a policy of flexibility in the economic system, reducing its own intervention and encouraging a system of free competition. For its part, private enterprise constitutes the most dynamic element. . . as we move into a more competitive climate."[11] Should not workers have the right to strike when business is privately owned and the quest for profits constitutes the chief motivation for employer activity? Is this not a fair and just component within a free enterprise system? The alternative reminds one of involuntary servitude. No matter how the Spanish government rationalizes the illegality of strikes, this stubborn fact remains--a government policy that outlaws strikes within a capitalistic free enterprise system is a travesty on social justice.

Needless to mention, Spain's prohibition of strikes violates a most basic doctrine of the International Labor Organization. In 1957, the General Conference of the International Labor Organization called "upon the government of the States Members of the International Labor Organization to take measures to abolish within the shortest possible time all laws and administrative regulations hampering or restricting the free exercise of trade union rights, to adopt laws, where this had not been done, ensuring the effective and unrestricted exercise of trade union rights, including the right to strike. . ."(Emphasis added) This ILO principle is contained in its resolution concerning "the Abolition of Anti-Trade Union Legislation in the States Members of the International Labor Organization." For Spain, this plea, of course, falls upon deaf ears. At this writing its government refuses to permit workers to strike for any purpose and under all conditions. At its pleasure, the Spanish government can apply the sternest penalties on striking workers. And so the most obvious violation of human, social, and economic rights exists. Working for private employers, Spanish workers, nevertheless, cannot take action to protest effectively against working conditions that they believe to be unjust.

---

[11]Summary of the Spanish Economic and Social Development Plan, 1964-1967, Commission of the Government Development Plan, Office of Public Relations, Madrid, 1964, pp. 14-15.

DISTRIBUTION OF NATIONAL INCOME

Another indicator of the effectiveness of the Spanish collective bargaining system is the distribution of the national income. That the Spanish workers have not fared equitably in this respect is even admitted by the Spanish government. Thus,

> Per capita income is not very high in our country [as of 1964, the per capita income amounted to about $385.00 per year]. The disparities in its distribution determine the imperious necessity to improve living conditions of the people of Spain. As regards functional distribution, it is noteworthy that among wage earners, 39.3 per cent receive 60.9 per cent of the [national] income while 60.7 per cent receive only 39.1 per cent. This disparity is still more acute in the distribution of average wages of the non-wage earning working population: while 85.1 per cent of the Spanish population received 57.5 per cent of the total, 14.6 shares 42.5 per cent. [12]

As presented above, during the operation of the 1958 law, there has been some improvement in the workers' comparative position in the Spanish economy. Real wages have increased by 30 per cent from 1960 to 1963. Still, as the Spanish government itself points out, the distribution of income is inequitable and a national disgrace. If the government recognizes this problem, how can one account for the 1964 wage control program? Surely, this program will sharpen the disparity between economic classes. It is unacceptable to argue that this wage policy is required to combat Spain's recent inflation. This problem can be dealt with by more effective means, for example, the curbing of monopoly within the nation. Despite the fact that the Spanish government is well aware of monopoly control of prices as an inflationary force, it does not undertake effective action to promote competition in the product market. There is no Spanish legislation comparable to the Sherman and Clayton Acts. Rather, it accepts monopoly as a fait accompli, and subordinates the interest of the Spanish workers to monopolistic interests.

----

[12] Ibid., p. 17.

FREE COLLECTIVE BARGAINING

If Spanish collective bargaining is evaluated on the basis of self-determination, the conclusion, of course, must be that it fails to measure up to the standards of free collective bargaining. That there is a measure of self-determination is conceded. Workers and employers may negotiate collective bargaining contracts and may adjust to their particular problems. That the 1958 law reflects an important shift in Spanish labor relations policy cannot be denied. However, as amply demonstrated, the collective bargaining system is operated under the fist of the Spanish government. Not only is the contract negotiated within the network of the state controlled Spanish Syndical Organization, which has, of course, no resemblance to free and independent labor unions, but the Spanish government through the Ministry of Labor has the ultimate power to approve or disapprove agreements, and, of course, serves as the arbitrator of unresolved disputes. No system of private arbitration is provided for in the application or construction of agreements, or for the determination of workers' complaints of contractual violations. There is no need to belabor this point. The fact is that the Spanish collective bargaining system fails to reflect those elements that are required for a free system of collective bargaining.

Even the Spanish government implicitly recognizes that its collective bargaining program fails to conform to those standards that distinguish a free or state uncontrolled system. Spain has never signed ILO Convention No. 98, adopted in 1949, concerning the "Application of the Principles of the Right to Organize and to Bargain Collectively." This fundamental ILO doctrine speaks in terms of a system which is divorced from state control. The Spanish system simply does not measure up to this standard.

CHAPTER 7 SPAIN'S LABOR POLICY: CONCLUSIONS

This volume has shown how labor relations are carried out in a totalitarian state that has made an effort to liberalize its institutions, including policies which bear upon the employer-employee relationship. On the basis of the analysis, the conclusion is irrefutable that within Spain the heritage of government control of labor relations far outweighs the elements of liberalization. In the light of the Spanish tradition of state control of labor relations and political totalitarianism, the element of liberalism might appear significant. Within this framework, the current state domination of labor relations may be understandable. Still, when judged on the basis of democratic standards, the Spanish labor relations system adds up to one of state control and domination. Indeed, the Spanish program of state control is a necessary corollary of the totalitarian structure of the Spanish state. Its elimination most likely would result in the collapse of the contemporary Spanish government. It is obvious that the current regime cannot bear the risk of a free system of collective bargaining, independent unions, and the right to strike.

In any event, Spain's system of reglamentaciones is still in effect; strikes are still illegal; and independent unions and employer associations are still unlawful. These stubborn facts outweigh the tendency of liberalization that is expressed in a government controlled system of collective bargaining and the Spanish government's recognition of collective conflicts. That Spain's labor relations policy contains more elements of freedom than was true before 1958 is conceded; however, this is only a relative condition, and the judgment must be that the state plays the predominant role in the shaping of labor relations policy.

The Spanish Syndical Organization from time to time has challenged the authority of the Ministry of Labor which is currently far more important than the syndical system in the determination of working conditions. For example, some officials of the Spanish Syndical Organization would strip the Ministry of Labor of its power to approve or disapprove collective bargaining agreements and of its power to serve as

the arbitrator whenever there exists an impasse in negotiations.   Also, there is some evidence that the syndical organization would abolish the current system of reglamentaciones
as now constituted.   If successful in this respect, the Ministry of Labor would have correspondingly less authority in the
labor relations field.   As expected, the Ministry of Labor op-
poses each and every one of these proposals, and, indeed,
wants greater power in the area of labor relations.   For example, as pointed out above, there is some thought in the Ministry of Labor that it should have the power to determine when
a collective bargaining negotiation should start.

These syndical suggestions should not be interpreted to
mean that employers and employees would then be free from
state control in the determination of working conditions if they
are translated into public policy.   In place of the current system of reglamentaciones, it is proposed that some other agency of the government would be authorized to put into effect minimum labor standards.   The powers now possessed by the Ministry of Labor over collective bargaining would undoubtedly be
claimed by the Spanish Syndical Organization.   In short, the
implementation of the syndical program would not mean that
employers and employees could then embark on a policy of
self-determination free from the controlling hand of the government.   As amply demonstrated, the Spanish Syndical Organization is an instrument of the state and will remain so as
long as its chief officers, the policy makers, are appointed
by the Spanish government and as long as employees and employers are forced to belong to it.   Through the network of
such appointed officials, the government can carry out predetermined policies as easily as it can through the Ministry of
Labor.   The question then is not whether Spain is to have a
system of authentic self-determination, but which agency will
implement government labor policy.   As far as the interests
of Spanish employers and employees are concerned, it does
not matter much whether this power is exercised by the Ministry of Labor or the Spanish Syndical Organization.   In either
case, they will not be the masters of their fate.

On the other hand, the struggle between the Ministry of
Labor and the Spanish Syndical Organization is of utmost importance to their top officials.   Though it is true that "empire
building" is a feature of any nation, the issue is far more important within a totalitarian state.   After all, Franco will not
live forever, and the mantle may fall to the government official who has aggrandized his power.   Though Spain's law of succession calls for a monarch to replace Franco, the royal ap-

pointee may very well be a figurehead, with real power being lodged in another person, say, a prime minister. Indeed, Mussolini's Italy was a nominal monarchy, and for a time Hitler's Germany was disguised as a constitutional form of government in which people elected a president. So, in its essence, the intergovernmental struggle between these two monolithic Spanish agencies is not a struggle to free labor relations from state control, but its outcome may determine Franco's replacement.

What of the future of Spanish labor relations? This writer sees no really fundamental change as long as Spain remains in its essence a totalitarian state. There may be a shift of power between government agencies, some procedural changes in the area of collective bargaining, perhaps some alterations in the structure of the Spanish Syndical Organization. However, these modifications, though they may be served up to the Spanish people as monumental changes of the utmost importance, in their essence will not result in the creation of independent labor unions and the right to strike. The furniture may be moved around, but the room will essentially remain the same. Only fundamental changes, such as independent unions, the effective use of the strike, and other elements of a free labor relations system, would bring Spain's labor relations program in line with the community of nations of the western world.

BIBLIOGRAPHY

Anuario Estadístico de España. Presidencia del Gobierno, Instituto Nacional de Estadística. Madrid, 1963 and 1964.

Blanco, Juan Eugenio. Estudio de Los Convenios Colectivos. Ministerio de Trabajo, Instituto Nacional de Previsión. Madrid, 1963.

Cachero, Luís Alfonso Martínez. Actualidad de La Emigración Española. Ministerio de Trabajo, Instituto Español de Emigración. Madrid, 1964.

Capacitación Sindical. Organización Sindical Española, Centro de Estudios Sindicales. Madrid, 1960.

Chacón, G. Bayón, and Botija, E. Pérez. Manual de Derecho del Trabajo. Madrid, 1964.

Convenios Colectivos Sindicales. Ministerio de Trabajo, Secretaría General Técnica. Madrid, 1958.

Discursos y Mensajes del Jefe del Estado, 1955-1959. Dirección General de Información, Publicaciones Española. Madrid, 1960.

General Regulations For Trade Union Elections. Spanish Trade Union Organization. Madrid, 1963.

Guia y Compendio de Los Convenios Colectivos en España. Asociación Para El Progreso de La Dirección. Madrid, 1962.

Leñero, José Pérez. Convenios Colectivos Sindicales: Doctrina y Legislación. Madrid, 1959.

Los Convenios Colectivos Sindicales en El Sector Agrario. Organización Sindical Española, Servicio de Información y Publicaciones Sindicales. Madrid, 1962.

Manual del Dirigente de Empresa. Organización Sindical Española, Vicesecretaria Nacional de Ordenación Económica. Madrid, 1964.

Obras Completas de José Antonio Primo de Rivera. Delegación de Prensa y Propaganda de Falange Española Tradicionalista y de Las J. O. N. S. Madrid, 1942.

Problemas de Personal. Acción Social Patronal. Madrid, 1960.

Summary of the Spanish Economic and Social Development Plan, 1964-1967. Commission of the Government Development Plan, Office of Public Relations. Madrid, 1964.

The Economic Development of Spain. International Bank for Reconstruction and Development. Baltimore: Johns Hopkins Press, 1963.

Articles

Arrufat, Jorge. "Huelgas en España," Jornal, Organo de Difusión Sindicalista, Organización Sindical Española, Servicio de Relaciones Exteriores, Madrid, No. 67 (March, 1958) and No. 75 (June-July, 1959).

"Ayudas Para Las Situaciones de Paro Por Reconversión de Industrias," Ministerio de Trabajo, Oficina de Divulgación, 1963.

Bedoya, Javier M. de. "La Experiencia Española de Los Convenios Colectivos," Cuadernos de Previsión Laboral, No. 18, 1963.

_____. "Retribución y Productividad en Los Convenios Colectivos," Revista de Política Social, Instituto de Estudios Políticos, Madrid, No. 55 (July, 1962).

"El Enlace Sindical," Organización Sindical Española, Vicesecretaria Nacional de Ordenación Social. Madrid, 1963.

Gallego, Emilio Torres. "El Diálogo en El Mundo del Trabajo," Cuadernos Para El Diálogo. Madrid, No. 10-11 (July-August, 1964).

Izquierdo, Manuel. "Despidos Libres, " Revista de Legislación Social. Madrid, No. 192 (October, 1959).

Jornal, Organo de Difusión Sindicalista, Organización Sindical Española, Servicio de Relaciones Exteriores. Madrid, No. 67 (March, 1958) and No. 80 (April-May, 1960).

"La Emigración Española a Europa, " Revista de Información del I. N. I. , Estudios Económicos, Información y Síntesis del Instituto, October, 1964.

"La Tendencia Salarial en Los Convenios Colectivos, " Organización Sindical Española, Vicesecretaria Nacional de Ordenación Social, June, 1964.

Leñero, José Pérez. "Convenios Colectivos Sindicales, " Revista de Trabajo, Ministerio de Trabajo, V. 7 (July, 1958), p. 3.

"Los Convenios Colectivos Sindicales de Trabajo en Las Actividades Agropecurias, " Jornal, Madrid, No. 80 (April-May, 1960).

"Magnífico Sentido Social de Un Convenio Colectivo, " Revista de Legislación Social, No. 221 (March, 1962).

Maravall, Héctor. "Las Negociaciones Colectivos, " Revista de Política Social, Instituto Estudios Políticos. Madrid, V. 57 (1963).

Martín, Jacinto. "Cincuenta Años de Vida Sindical, " Cuadernos Para El Diálogo. Madrid, No. 9 (June, 1964).

Mejias, Pedro Lamata. "El Sindicato y La Contratación Laboral, " Jornal, V. 80 (April-May, 1960).

Miranda, José Alvarez de. "Conflictos Colectivos Laborales, " Cuadernos, Organización Sindical Española, Centro de Estudios Sindicales. Madrid, No. 20 (June, 1963).

Norte, Francisco. "Convenios Colectivos Sindicales, " Revista de Trabajo, Ministerio de Trabajo. Madrid, V. 10 (October, 1958).

Official Bulletin. International Labor Office. Geneva, V. 47, No. 3, Supplement II (July, 1964).

Revista de Legislación Social. No. 22 (April, 1962).

Revista de Trabajo. Ministerio de Trabajo. Madrid, No. 3 (June, 1962).

Ricoi, Julian Ariza. "Convenios Colectivos," Cuadernos Para El Diálogo. Madrid, No. 10-11 (July-August, 1964).

Ros, José Manuel Mateu de. "El Convenio Colectivo, Instrumento de Unidad y Convivencia," Jornal, No. 80 (April - May, 1960).

Spain's American Weekly. Madrid: Guidepost Publications, November 6, 1964.

Tiempo Nuevo. Madrid, V. 10, No. 121 (May, 1964).

Torres, Francisco Giménez. "The Objectives of Spanish Unions," Organización Sindical Española, Servicio de Relaciones Exteriores Sindicales. Madrid, 1962.

"Trade Union Elections," National Assembly of Trade Union Elections, Spanish National Syndical Organization. Madrid, 1963.

Newspapers

ABC (Madrid), October 15, 1964.

Arriba (Madrid), November 1, 1964.

Christian Science Monitor, June 28, 1965.

El Alcazar (Madrid), November 20, 1964.

Hoja del Lunes (Madrid), October 5, 1964.

La Nueva España (Ovedio), September 14, 1964.

New York Times (American Edition), October 25, 1964; October 28, 1964.

Pueblo (Madrid), November 21, 1964.

Solidaridad Nacional (Barcelona), October 4, 1964.

Valladolid (Valladolid), October 2, 1964.

Ya (Madrid), November 7, 1962; March 26, 1964; September 4,
    1964; October 20, 1964; November 1, 1964; November 6,
    1964; November 10, 1964; November 20, 1964; November 24, 1964.